Walter Blackburn Harte

Meditations In Motley

A Bundle Of Papers Imbued With The Sobriety Of Midnight

Walter Blackburn Harte

Meditations In Motley
A Bundle Of Papers Imbued With The Sobriety Of Midnight

ISBN/EAN: 9783744651721

Printed in Europe, USA, Canada, Australia, Japan

Cover: Foto ©ninafisch / pixelio.de

More available books at **www.hansebooks.com**

MEDITATIONS IN MOTLEY

A BUNDLE OF PAPERS
IMBUED WITH THE SO-
BRIETY OF MIDNIGHT

By WALTER BLACKBURN HARTE

THE ARENA PUBLISHING
COMPANY, BOSTON, MASS.
MDCCCXCIV

" Motley's the only wear."
—*As You Like It.*

"I am now of all humours, that have show'd themselves humours, since the old days of goodman Adam to the pupil age of this present twelve o'clock at midnight."
—*Prince Henry in King Henry IV.*

CONTENTS.

OF the essays included in this unpreten-
tious bundle, one or two first saw the light
in the most unexpected and obscure corner
of a somewhat obscure parochial register,
under the general caption of " In A Corner at Dodsley's." Others have appeared
in different periodicals. I am indebted to
the Editor of the Arena for permission to
reprint the paper on " Prejudice."

I first took down the shutters at
Dodsley's, in October, 1891, in the
darkest, poorest, dismallest alley-way in
all Grub street, and for over two years I
was to be found there by all those who cared
to adventure in the literary slums. I chose
the name partly out of a contradictory
humor, my shop being situated so very far
away from Pall Mall, where Robert Dodsley's smart bookshop stood in Pope's and
Dr. Johnson's day, and partly because obscurity and squalor are forever associated
with the attractions of antiquarianism, and I

could only hope in such a quarter to attract the curious. A certain literary bum-bailiff, who objected to my existence and occupations upon principle, finally put the shutters up one fine winter morning, and I found employment elsewhere.

The papers as printed in the parochial register, were written, under some stress of circumstance, to arrest the attention of curious people and interest them in the merits of quack medicines, face powders, sauces and sewing machines. One or two, selected from a considerable number, are now hazarded in this new form without those adventitious aids to circulation.

If I could only hope to see this little venture prosper half as well as do some of the quack medicines, I should be reconciled to the Fates — and I should not disturb my peace of mind with any unnecessary inquiries into the effects of the syllabub, nor the expert criticisms which might be made upon it.

I had no idea of formally dedicating this book to any one of my friends, because it occurred to me that it might be a dubious compliment, since Grub Street is in such bad odor; but on sober second thoughts I have finally decided to offer a tentative word by way of dedication. The opportunity to ingratiate myself with the judicious is too rare to be put aside for a doubt; I therefore commend this little book to the Devil and Dame Chance, the two most potent deities in literary fortunes as in all other sublunary dispensations.

WALTER BLACKBURN HARTE.

OCTOBER, 1894.
BOSTON, MASS.

ON CERTAIN

SATISFACTIONS OF PREJUDICE.

MEDITATIONS IN MOTLEY.

ON CERTAIN SATISFACTIONS OF PREJUDICE.

OVER a cup of tea and the evening paper I am constantly informed by the delightful old lady, who sits at the end of the board and gravely and quietly replenishes my cup without any demur until the limit of five cups is reached, when neither prayers, threats nor entreaties will induce her to pour out another drop, that I am a person of violent antipathies and prejudices. When I attempt to remonstrate and clear myself of this dreadful charge, by explaining that any splenetic explosions in which I may occasionally indulge at the table are imbued with the high moral purpose of shaking the company out of their immoral apathy, I only make matters worse. As the lady absolutely refuses to read anything more exciting than Paley's

"Moral Philosophy," I cannot convince
her of the wanton wickedness of her contemporaries, especially such of them as
write in the newspapers; and I pen this, I
hope scientific, analysis of that cerebral
irritation which is called prejudice under
this roof, and a glimpse of the subject of
prejudice in general, in the hope that discussion of the paper over the tea table
will lift a gloom from my social character
that has rested upon it in Miss Paulina
Pinckney's mind these many years.

At the other end of the table (years of
happy and memorable tea-table strife have
given me the place of honor at her right
hand, formerly occupied by a famous psy-
chologist possessed with a strong intellectual partiality for criminals), there sits a
young man who manufactures what is
called editorial opinion for the *Sentinel;*
and our prim but tender-hearted hostess
declares that a malicious curiosity once
prompted her to read that valuable organ
of opinion, but respect for her lodger pre-
vailed over her worser instincts; for, truth
to tell, the young man is really quite ordi-
narily behaved and, up to this time of
writing, has never been discovered at any-

body's keyhole or under anybody's bed or
concealed in anybody's clothes closet.
Miss Paulina has him under constant sur-
veillance, though, in spite of her scruples
of conscience, and she had grave doubts
about allowing the associate of criminals
to have a latch key. She believes he has
a hand in every murder mystery that gets
into the air. She is convinced the newspaper press is the invention of the Devil,
and will not give it any of her countenance.
I am not orthodox, but I share Miss Paulina's conviction. I most sincerely uphold
the good lady's resolution in abjuring the
Sentinel, and I think it reflects great credit
upon her character. And then I know
that not everybody in this world can suffer
to have their illusions comparatively exam-
ined, and cheerfully feel that they are
gainers; as they actually are, since added
to their original stock of illusions, they
acquire a knowledge of realities. It is certainly better for the manufacturer of editorial opinion that Miss Paulina extends to
him this dubious charity, for if he is re-
sponsible for any of the *Sentinel's* opinions
he is to be pitied for enjoying so much of
his own society.

The young man himself, however, smiles whimsically at my occasional explosions of splenetic disgust. He has, in fact, some humor and discrimination, and he never reads the *Sentinel*. Now I do, because the doctor tells me exercise is good for my liver, and I think it stirs me up a bit to damn the *Sentinel* now and then. I know the *Sentinel* man is not hurt, for he really has so much appreciation of good literature that his table is piled high with the spoil of my bookshelves; and besides, he knows I too have been a brigand, and a mutual antipathy has drawn us together. But our good gray landlady belongs to a more sober and strenuous time; there is a good deal of the old Puritan conscience in her; and she cannot understand that our journalistic friend experiences a strange joy in bearing all possible odium for a trade he loathes, but being a canny, cautious soul, dares not damn with my whole-souled ardor.

It is because I permit myself the fullest satisfaction of my antipathies that I am able to get along with fewer distractions than most of my less prodigal associates, who have to be penurious of their true

opinions to provide for the indulgence of
their luxurious tastes. For this reason,
my good landlady sometimes suspects me
of hypocrisy. She contrasts my general
opinions, which are tolerant enough, with
my ebullitions on certain subjects — undertaken sometimes for the sake of getting
rid of an honest opinion and sometimes for
my liver — of which, on paper, I am quite
prepared to see both sides, but over the
tea table, to pleasure myself, will only see
one, and she cannot reconcile my ideas on
hygiene with her beautiful belief in the
practicability of the Beatitudes.

I have sometimes tried to explain to the
good lady, that, it being admitted, as it
must be admitted, that every man having
so much original sin, a good stock of vigorous abstract prejudices is essential to
afford any room for the development of a
few virtues. She does not follow my rea-
soning, and I honestly believe she harbors
a dread suspicion that a sixth cup of tea
any evening might excite me to the commission of some awful atrocity — perhaps
the murder of the editorial opinion-maker
of the *Sentinel*.

The fact is my prejudices afford me my

greatest relaxation, a good heated, unspar-
ing tea-table argument, in which I conceive
there is no excitement or stimulant unless
one is notoriously on the wrong side, with
some cherished prejudices in peril to warm
one up for the strife, and make defeat
more glorious than any cold-blooded vic-
tory of mere logic. A man who does not
possess certain well recognized and very
dear prejudices, for which he will fight
against a whole roomful of bloodthirsty
opponents, is in very great danger in more
serious crises of not being aware of certain
congenital errors of mind, which are perfectly familiar to his friends; and not only
that, but does any one believe such a man
would run any risk for the maintenance of
any moral conviction whatsoever? Such a
man is too lukewarm and cautious to love
the truth. It may seem paradoxical, but
to always prefer logic to a good wholesome
prejudice is enough to make one suspect
such a man would not stick at perjury.
This is one of the advantages of acquiring
a sympathetic acquaintance with the whole
range of one's prejudices.

But the most cogent argument for a due
recognition of them in one's social life is

that they are really more sociable and loquacious than logic and reason, which are often uncharitable and brutal, if not cold and glum. And to recognize one's prejudices also argues the possession of a logical faculty of some utility, for the half of education is to be able to sift the most palpable errors out of one's knowledge, and live within one's intellectual income without any dangerous pretension, making such of one's errors and prejudices as have any attribute of picturesqueness about them, serve some innocent social purpose, so that in every society one need not become absolutely bankrupt in twenty-four hours.

Behind my evening paper, and in the middle of my fourth cup of Oolong, I would consider it unsocial and, if the term may be allowed, pedantic, to suddenly get becalmed in some unescapably logical conclusion, when all the rest of the company was unbent and familiar, and when I could perhaps add to the general gaiety, as well as exhilarate my sluggish pulse, by waging a passionate battle for some good old antiquated prejudice, probably inherited from a great grandfather addicted to snuffing and proverbial philosophy. My only relapses into purely unexceptionable rational moods at the tea table, occur when I see the bottom of my fifth cup, and all my logic rises for a futile appeal to that implacable moralist, who does not hesitate to avow her conviction that a drop over my allowance would precipitate me upon a literary career of corrupting the young. I hope this consideration has due weight with me — but I confess to a strong prejudice concerning this literary tenderness for the young.

I have in this way developed a sort of intellectual incredulity, which, while making me tender toward my prejudices, keeps me from becoming arrogant over my reasoned opinions. The knowledge of how very specious and satisfactory the one may be, saves me from being over credulous about the others. I sometimes suspect, too, that some of the finest webs of logic are spun to uphold the most fantastic and palpable sophistries; and so in the passionate championing of my prejudices, I honestly think that I have acquired a portion of that humility which will cling to its heart and soul convictions in spite of con-

tumely and persecution. This indulgent
incredulity in regard to the credulousness
of my nature, which would fain turn some
of these hopes into facts, gives me a sort
of humorous interest in those very facts,
which would come very harshly upon me
but for this appreciation of the true nature
of my illusions. I grant I have some prejudice against the facts, in a good many
instances, but being undeceived about my
own prejudices, which have much greater
claims upon my regard, I mitigate something of their harshness by not attaching
to them quite so much importance as some
more equable and more credulous persons
do.

Thus while the more matter-of-fact of
my friends have forfeited all their illusions
before reaching the age of thirty, I hope to
retain a sufficiently large number of amusing prejudices to exercise and keep me in
humor for a lifetime; and that without
becoming seriously a victim of my own
illusions. So my incredulity, being of a
slow and native growth — it was of almost
unconscious development until my plunge
into the study of psychology — has not
destroyed and deprived me of the advan-

tages of any prejudices that a kind Providence and the concomitance of education
and early surroundings ordained should
be mine, as contributory to my social happiness; but it has maintained an equilib-
rium between the real world and the world
of my illusions, which I cannot but think
has not only been of material benefit to
me in my earthly pilgrimage, but has
afforded me much innocent mirth at my
own expense, when I was too desperately
poor to indulge in laughter at anybody
else's. And truly the man who cannot
laugh heartily at the unescapable discrep-
ancy between his conscience and his
inclinations, who cannot perceive the ludicrousness of his grave and sober part, be
it what it may, in this great farce of a
world, cannot have much charity for those
who, either from indolence or natural unfit-
ness, or an excess of philosophic temperament, fail to get anything out of the
scramble but hard knocks.

Here is the advantage of boldly acknowl-
edging one's prejudices to oneself (not to
the undiscriminating who judge men upon
their small talk and small change): it gives
one a juster conception of the extent of

one's capital ideas and knowledge, and
leaves illusions more or less separate and
distinct for the safe employment of one's
hours of relaxation. Even if one has to
abandon some of one's most sober and
complacent parts of knowledge in this process of sifting, in the certain gain of prejudices one must increase in both knowledge
and tolerance. And through the practice
of this discrimination and economy, one
can put both one's knowledge and one's
prejudices out at interest, and win men's
good opinion in business and in social life,
without being compelled to do them so
much injury as men do who obey their
prejudices from greed or ambition without
any system or comprehension. I think
most people have no idea of the social utility of a good stock of prejudices. In the
agreeable strife of the tea table one can
really be much wittier in defence of one's
most monstrous prejudices than in the
calm and sober attempt to gain a hearing
for really substantial and rational opinions
on church and state. But then I have a
theory that no man or woman entirely
lacking in wit and humor should dare to
nourish any prejudices — or if they must,

they should only do so in a monastic silence and secrecy. Those of us who enjoy the advantage of the society of witty women know how much their prejudices contribute to their charm and brilliancy. Thus by informing myself upon my pet credulities, I have not merely not shattered my illusions, but I have acquired some sympathy for the flattering prejudices of others. At the same time I am wary and cautious, and I enjoy the luxury of cherishing my prejudices without becoming the spoil of my enemies. The man who confuses his prejudices with his moral or immoral convictions is apt either to be a petty tyrant, or the prey of all those large souls who fatten upon others' moral convictions, but with such incorruptible consciences that they fear no contamination.

For instance, I have a prejudice against the Calvinistic theory of total depravity, although my reason, appalled with the facts, rebels; but strong and persistent as is the prejudice, my mental habit of final dubiousness preserves me in the imminent peril of a fatal delusion, that might unfit me for the social state into which I was most unexpectedly born. I have luckily

sufficient tolerance for worldly wisdom to
save me from allowing what may only be
a most ungrounded prejudice to precipitate
me into any dangerous sapiency of philanthropy, that, in all probability, would
quickly land me in the fearful quagmire of
being helplessly dependent upon the chance
of the same delusion seizing upon others;
and introspection has convinced me that
any real love and tenderness is a quality
or condition of mind which is daily menaced with too many ugly realities to be at
all stable and constant. The one compensation for this fact is that the greatest
charity is tolerance in all matters of social
and philosophic opinion, which only
attracts the best and finest natures and
has no fascination for those wasps of
humanity that embarrass and prey upon all
philanthropy but that which invariably
suggests itself to the mind in inverted
commas — in the secure keeping of shrewd
managers of "charity" organizations. All
other so-called practical charity that has
not this salt of heroic fundamental sanity
and justice is the most villainous of
mummeries. It demands higher qualities
to declare justice in spite of all "respect-

able " opinion than to give mere money or bricks. "But money is a good soldier, sir, and will on."

Thus I cannot escape the conviction (although I should like to, as I must oppose conscience when it pricks me to acknowledge an obligation which may seem to more positive minds a vice) that in this one respect I have been somewhat exceptionally fortunate; for though I have many friends and a wide circle of acquaintances, and, as far as my knowledge goes, but few of them are in such destitute circumstances as to be wholly lacking in prejudices, I do not think many of them experience any genuine thrill of pleasure when the certainty is borne in upon them — if that ever happens — that some of their most tenaciously held opinions are in indubitable opposition to facts. It may be scouted as an unreasonable opinion, but half the pleasure of possessing fantastic prejudices consists in being unescapably convicted of error at the end of an argument; for in this conviction is a delicate tribute to one's power of logical construction even with admitted disabilities. I cannot help reflecting, although in this connection it may sound ominously like self-complacency, that men with such cold sympathies that they will not boldly father their prejudices must ever shut out of their minds either something of error or of truth; and it seems to me our capacities as well as our opportunities for obtaining innocent pleasures in this sad old world, are not sufficiently great to justify a prudent man in practising such penury and inhospitality.

I maintain that the man who cannot and dare not admit that the other party to an argument—I am excluding politics, economics and all sober questions but philosophy, which affords the most magnificent opportunities to fantastical souls—has the preponderance of evidence and facts, and still cling courageously to his more picturesque or more agreeable prejudices, is sadly lacking in moral stamina, and is not of that stuff out of which heroes and martyrs are made. If one can only manage it, there is something more comforting in the conviction of infant damnation or the eternal torments of those pagans who do not share our theological fiddle-de-dee than in all the chilly assurances of mere reason. But on the other hand, in a charity that

includes dreadful errors of all sorts you
have all the real moral progress of civilization, the measure of every man — tolerance
of opinion, which surely, to escape all possible charges of hypocrisy and invidious
distinctions, must include charity to self.
We should reconcile ourselves to our
errors with the thought that, granting all
the great beacons of the ages, a perfectly
balanced mind does not exist. There is
some fatal fixity of ideas in even the greatest minds, that must exclude much sanity.
Besides, a great deal of modern sober
inquiry is being directed to a reëxamina-
tion of ancient misses at truth.

In considering prejudices in a broad
and tolerant spirit, and the satisfactions it
is possible to derive from them, one should
certainly turn to Sir Thomas Browne. As
the author of a most learned work on
"Vulgar Errors," and the "Religio Medici," he has won the good will of a posterity of bookish men through the possession
of a goodly share of the most delicious
whimsies and prejudices. It will be
remembered that he was concerned with
Sir Matthew Hale in the burning of
witches, a fact which, while I try to cherish

the most humane sentiments, I cannot but think contributes something to my delight in his opinions. "The extreme age of an opinion seemed to him to be some warrant for its truth"; and this tendency of mind opened up a field of sober humor and fine-spun disputations in these philosophic meditations on life and destiny and faith and death, more rich in suggestive error and flashes of illuminative truth, proving some unprovable hypothesis, than one can find in any body of fantastical speculation within the same compass in the whole range of English literature. But of course the "Religio Medici" is alone in its kind.

If one is of Sir Thomas Browne's way of thinking that "It is too late to be ambitious," then one can all the more cheerfully congratulate oneself upon a store of robust prejudices for companionship in the swift changing years, and the isolation of one's age. Even the best of wives is not so constant as a well-grounded prejudice; and sons and daughters notoriously grow from short frocks into indifference, and ultimately knŏw only our whimsies and not us. If we can but learn to recognize our prejudices we are saved from loneliness.

It is improbable, however, that many can
endure to live in such a penury of complacency, to put the matter on no higher
grounds, and so the unwisdom of ambition
in this late day will probably never shame
a newly-reached majority out of its beady
cups; and in this, as in most other things,
Nature conspires against reason. But
there can surely be no better admonition
than Sir Thomas Browne's to those who,
being blessed with the most happy prejudices, are so ill-advised and so injudicious
as to poison their happiness and contentment with a mad desire to propagate them.
These gifts, whether from Providence or the
Devil, should be their own reward; it is
prodigal to squander them in the reckless
gambling of vanity. Browne says, "Those
have not only depraved understandings, but
diseased affections, which cannot enjoy a
singularity without a heresy, or be the
author of an opinion without they be of a
sect also."

There is a goodly number of most delightful writers (though the most of them
lie in the cemeteries) who scorn to use the
arts of the politician and of the multitude
of scribblers, only happy in some larger

shadow than their own, who still hope to get a currency upon the popular tongue by combatting and banning in a grandeur of fantastic and isolated opinion all those popular notions that good, respectable men inherit and apparently carry in their pockets (for they do not truly concern their heads), as good Catholics carry their rosaries. The danger for some of these men is that when they finally become aware of the desperately unintelligent and irrelevant character of a great deal of "wisdom," they are apt to become slothfully content with a scepticism of mere wit. That is not the worst of it with men who lack wit. A prejudice without wit is the Devil with gout — all prescriptions fail to meet the case. With the progress of time some of the finest fantastic spirits not infrequently seem to abdicate reason altogether for the indulgence of their prejudices, because they consider the former to be too common among men, while the latter, in their very vigor and hardiness, and the opposition and clamor they sometimes provoke, give their possessors a peculiar sense of innate originality. Perhaps, with all the mountains of literature behind us,

all the originality possible for us moderns
lies in our prejudices.   In reading some of
my contemporaries I think this must be so.
The persons just alluded to would rather
be removed, even through the very prepos-
terousness of their errors, from the ordinary mass of men, than be lost in the miry
darkness of some general opinion of "common sense," which philosophy tells them
— and herein is some justification to balance, if not to top, their vanity — may be
proved, a generation or so hence, to be
quite as unsubstantial, though without any
redeeming quality of picturesqueness.

The great majority of men are easily
seduced from their native thoughts by the
ambition to rise in some party or win popular applause, and to achieve this success
they have to concur in prejudices whose
nativity could scarcely recommend them to
noble minds.   There are other men who,
in the uncertainty of knowledge, are,
above all, desirous of maintaining some
sort of intellectual integrity, and they naturally reject all those monstrous popular
prejudices, stamped with the "judicial
authority," as having no avowed and
decent parentage, which would give some

clue to nature, as an honest individual prejudice sometimes does; these hold their
own prejudices on probation, as being perhaps after all scarcely less dubious than
much of the wisdom of theology and politics and moral and other philosophy. The
average minds, of course, do not understand them, and mediocrities without a
peck more of reason, and with a destitution
of wit, laugh them to scorn; for the majority of men are lacking in the vigor of
mind necessary to the creation, by illogical
thinking, of a lusty native prejudice, and
their opinions, like their prayers, are made
for them. The masses, whose sole thinking is the morning's hot politics, are in a
revolt against any communism of bread
and meat, for political economists have
shown them the brazen and wicked folly of
assuming that these things were intended
by Nature to supply her own turbulent
claims in empty stomachs; but they are
nevertheless for the most part divided in
their opinions and their morals more as
clamorous, unthinking communes than as
individuals, and only a few heretics outside
the communes know where the mechanism
of all these staid opinions is to be found,

and what and whose purposes it serves.
The masses of men do not think except
through the symbols provided for them.
It is no reproach to them, for their bellies
are in pawn to a conspiracy against the
welfare of the race. One cannot but think
that perhaps if all men clung courageously
to their prejudices we might enjoy a greater
sanity of public opinion than we do in the
universal adoration of the "judicial character"; and in all the realistic concerns of
life we would possibly gain in tenderness
and charity.

These few heretical writers who glory in
their native prejudices, but unfortunately
too often lose, in the battle of opinions, a
wholesome and necessary sub-conscious
scepticism about them, are often nearer to
Nature in emptying their minds without
hypocrisy, than the majority of writers,
who pay more court to judicial ignorance
than they do to the acquisition of knowledge. And moreover they are, if one
reads them in the right spirit, more amusing than some other graver and less erratic
writers. We do not go to them when we
are lost in the mazes of life, but for an
after-dinner pill they are amazingly good

homœopathists. And they serve at least one purpose; they are the nipping east wind of all that good, "respectable" opinion that sets one's teeth on edge. They wage war upon all wicked self-complacency — but their own; and, of course, we can only expect a philosophy that would include the latter from very rare humorists indeed. Nor would such be likely to take their prejudices with so much of seriousness as the sort of persons I have in mind. Job had this inclusive quality of wisdom, but he could scarcely have derived the same amount of pleasure from his prejudices as the modern writers I am hinting at, whose ambition is not prophecy or exhortation, but the sort of heresy which inspires as much amiable mirth as anger. Like all schismatics it is only their wit saves them from being bigots. It is the lack of wit that makes all sorts and conditions of orthodox folk so desperately dull. How can one be witty in a world about which one has made up one's mind once and forever? Each day must bring the most unendurable monotony to the orthodox who never fear any doubts lurking round the corner.

But the great peril of men of this fine fanatic temperament is that they often grow tired of the isolated grandeur of amusing the dull with paradoxes too subtle for comprehension at a glance, and not grave enough to interest the wise who have learned to suspect their vanities, and resolve to put their paradoxes into a system. From being too erratic to long occupy any one province of thought they settle down into a persistence of contradiction that is often finally disastrous to their wit. Some petty accident, or a new and sudden influence at the critical period of life, throws them from incertitude, expressed in genially held prejudices, into a fury of positivism, and they seek to turn what was an amiable and amusing folly, in the consideration of men of discernment, into the alarming form of "a school" of folly. This gives an edge to the pointless ribaldry of the dull, who cannot appreciate a quip for its own sake, and have no sense of the sobriety of true humor; the sort of plaguy villains who drive a rational, thinking being mad in twenty-four hours' enforced society with their coagulated nonsense and utterly unreasonable "common sense." And yet perhaps in a world of fine wits it might be possible, and not so menacing, to see the prosperity of all sorts of fantastic "schools"—just for the quip's sake; but in a stupid "common sense" world we can hope for no such mitigation of our evil state. The old philosophy of laughter seems to have gone out of fashion. Therefore we must warn Launcelot, in the words of Sir Thomas Browne, against the perils of this adventure. So long as the world is wedded to common sense it cannot contain much philosophy, or be a very comfortable place for those whose opinions cannot find an echo at every fish wife's basket in the market place.

An old prejudice is like an old friend. We see it often in reason's stuffy police court, and hearing that dread sentence passed upon it by judge and jury, we may in very shame abjure it; but it will as likely as not turn up again, and again be welcomed and pressed into the breach in some tea-table battle. And then, too, the introspectively-minded man, who has something like an illustrated biography of his mind since childhood's earliest memories, knows that there is some difference in prejudices. The latest prejudice, created by some newspaper report, some chance word, some jar to one's interests, cannot hold its own with one of those prejudices that have persisted from childhood. An old prejudice will flare up under a hint of the old excitement in the sunset of life, when all the other prejudices have long faded out of mind. The passing fickle prejudices may have laid waste a world, but at the end of life they shrink into insignificance. The only prejudices that linger then are those old ones that used to set the table in a roar — one's congenital, childish prejudices. The "broad minded" man often has just as many prejudices as the old fogy — and one of them is a prejudice against the idea of their universal distribution. As a man prospers, many of his widening interests in what appears to him to be a larger social world are but new prejudices: thus a man gets the slang of clubs, the *patois* of "society," the "wisdom" of moneyed men, the narrow cant of schools of ethics supported and encouraged by the idle and fashionable classes, and he feels that life is growing richer and richer for him. In reality the process is reversed. In a continual surrender of his own native habits of thought he is growing poorer and poorer.

·Ten new prejudices cannot produce that satisfaction which makes one grapple the lifelong companion to one's soul with hooks of steel. The old prejudice may cause less concern than a new one, but it confers more responsibility, and it is necessary to exercise more energy and feeling to protect it. Some of the lighter prejudices of social exigency but need some mishap in a bargain, some change of fortunes or some accidental acquaintance or book to disturb them; they come and go and are scattered with the beady philosophy of life that gave them sanction. But one's radically inherent prejudices are not so much the creation of hope and vanity and pride, as mysterious and oftentimes wise and tender admonitors of the conscience, warning it, in spite of all judicial authority, experience, worldly precepts and example, all respectable opinion, to cling to something of the old unquestioning pity and mercy and charity. Let pride drive on with its superior airs, as it throws a silver coin with scarcely a glance to the beggar on the highway; old prejudice, which cares not for social opinion and laughs at it, turns out of the road into the path and sits down to loaf and chat with a human being. That is prejudice of the right sort. Pride is but prejudice; but how often those who have known misery in youth think it necessary to rob Chance of her part of their prosperity to bolster up their vanity. But the wiser man thanks the goddess of Chance, who may strip him and his at the eleventh hour, and clings to the old prejudice that in youth warned, that to love some men merely for their abilities and capacities, and to despise others for their lack of them, was simply to alternately fawn upon and spurn Mother Nature, who is indifferent to our love or hate. The pride that shuns and scoffs at the simple merely denies itself an acquaintance with one of the most tolerable and sometimes tender of Nature's aspects. A good sceptical prejudice against the pretensions of all human wisdom will counteract this temptation to live in an atmosphere of chill complacency; it is because the wise are so seldom deceived with their wisdom that we so frequently find them, as we read their biographies, sitting on the benches in the alehouses listening to the talk of the simple. The old prejudice of youth against the authority that would narrow and pen up its heaven and earth is a true instinct; we are wisest in the untroubled paganism of childhood, when we do not doubt that all wonder and beauty and mystery is part of our inheritance; and that man is wisest who can cling, in the clash of new prejudices, to the old prejudice so closely woven into the old illusions and enthusiasms of youth. In outgrowing the latter, if one can but cling to the prejudice one is preserving something also of the faith of childhood.

It was ignorance that dreamed of heaven and fairyland; though it was cunning that threw wide open the gates and gave the poor heaven forever while it seized upon earth. But while the mass of us have always been tenants at will upon earth, under most tyrannous sub-landlords, we have never been formally dispossessed of heaven — although a good many of us are a little anxious to obtain some more secure title to a share of the earth and its fruits, since we cannot bring heaven to earth. But we are told we have arrived too late —

the earth and its benefits were divided up about a thousand years ago, and only heaven is left to us; and so perhaps after all we owe more to ignorance than we do to wisdom. Some of us have a prejudice against this apportionment of heaven and earth, and especially as we are menaced with a new peril; we see the temples raised on every hand in which Plutus, invoking all the wondrous wisdom of priestcraft, is trying to placate our God and get into heaven. Since wisdom has made us so incontrovertibly superfluous on God's earth, where all the authority and learning shows our error in coming a thousand years late, what sort of guarantee have we that we may not yet be dispossessed of heaven by the same weight of judicial authority?

Ah, but heaven is God's domain, says the gentleman in cassock and gown. Of course, sir, but whose is the earth? Is not that God's, too? We have a prejudice against the weighty authority which has dispossessed us here and made us trespassers whichever way we turn; and since one of the most learned of the white-choker profession, a certain Dr. Malthus, announced that we were born too late, that there were no plates laid for us at Nature's banquet, that we had no right to persist in an existence conferred upon us by accident and should betake ourselves off this planet, we have a prejudice against you torch bearers who may be luring us, like Cornwall wreckers, to our destruction. We hear you declaiming a strange "Christian" gospel to our taskmasters that sounds familiarly like their fantastic political economy, and we openly suspect you of a collusion to shut us out of heaven itself. I am sorely afraid we shall find Plutus in possession, and shall doubtless be told by Dr. Malthus: "Too late, too late; everything was apportioned a thousand years ago. There are no more places at the banquet here." Ah, yes, we must confess to a sad prejudice against you soft-pawed, white-choker creature, for since we cannot reverse the law of gravitation, you have greatly helped to make it sorely difficult for us to breathe anywhere without some guilty trespass.

It may be indeed no idle fancy that we are too late to dream of heaven, since wisdom claims to hold its golden keys; but there are pagan joys still left to us in fairy-

land, and let us as long as possible cling
to these with a tender prejudice. Learning has given us little happiness; let ignorance disclose the reason, though it comes
to the block for so doing—it is almost entirely oblivious of wisdom, which does not
need so many granaries, but only eyes and
hearts. Ignorance in giving us fairyland
has made us some compensation for the
world it has shut us out of. We can only
preserve it by cherishing our prejudices.
Once let us admit to ourselves the dreadful deception of our prejudices, and in this
too crowded world we are desolate indeed
—companionless, and without a single illusion, the prey of a despair that admits of
none of that community of woe that makes
those, upon whose bounty we cringe, willing to endure the thought of the possibility
of sharing heaven with us. For Plutus
too has his ills—ennui, satiety, gout and
Bright's disease. And then what treas-
ures can exorcise doubt? It pursues us
all, rich or poor. But if it be true that
Charon expects no more from Alexander
than from Lazarus, we may perhaps indulge the prejudice that our white-choker
brethren are far too wise to escape their

due proportion of error, and so we may still find consolation in the hope that, if there is any after life, the Almighty will waive any consideration of our prejudice against Dr. Malthus and the rest, upon the ground of justification. We surely pay dearly enough in this world for our error of coming into it; and our obstinacy in remaining, in spite of all the disabilities, has in it, to my mind, something of heroism. We remain because we have a prejudice against God's vicegerents, the rightful owners; and there really is some satisfaction in the thought that while wisdom may harass and pinch and starve us, it cannot exorcise us — it cannot reverse the law of gravitation in our special behoof.

Our minor prejudices are too numerous for anything like adequate enumeration, and, since they increase with their satisfaction, they cannot be touched by mathematics. They are woven into the texture of all theology, philosophy, history, literature — everything. It was probably due to some congenital prejudice in John Calvin that we owe the five cardinal points of Calvinism, which my prejudices would sometimes have true, and at other times clamor

against.   But Calvin's bilous eye gave posterity something to wax witty over — and
that is enough of achievement for any man
who would benefit mankind.

The satisfaction that most people derive
from that prejudice called " patriotism " is
one of the most instructive things in this
world to any man who, before aspiring to
wisdom, is curious to know something of
the boundaries of folly.   This prejudice,
that lacks the redeeming qualities of others
I have in mind, is well characterized by
Schopenhauer, who, however, did not realize as fully as he might have done the possible disaster of robbing any man of the
sole satisfaction of his vanity.   He said:
"The cheapest sort of pride is national
pride; for if a man is proud of his own
nation, it argues that he has no qualities of
his own of which he can be proud; other-
wise, he would not have recourse to those
which he shares with so many millions of
his fellow-men."   But while some sort of
illusion is necessary to life, it must be
doubted if this peculiar prejudice serves
any useful purpose.

Perhaps   the   most   permanent   and
most widespread prejudice, and the one

which all men of contrary prejudices
should investigate carefully, is that against
men who publish unpleasant truths. The
history of government, philosophy, religion,
science and literature is occupied with
showing how much weighty wisdom has
been expended in stoning and crucifying
and broiling and frying the perverse and
wicked souls who were possessed of a prejudice in favor of their own wicked opinions and the truth. It is too much of a
subject for this paper — which is mainly
concerned with the general matter of the
satisfactions to be derived from those
smaller prejudices that have a social value.
These are such prejudices as the ancient
one against poverty, which cuts some people off from much good society, the prejudice against cynics and other folk with no
genius for hypocrisy, against honesty,
against old-fashioned ideas and new virtues, ancient truth and new books, poets
and critics, justice and mercy. The list,
if prolonged, would become a catalogue of
all the virtues, though it would also include
a fair proportion of vices.

But although it is the way of the world
to confuse all good things with prejudices,

(and we have here, to indulge a humor, somewhat acquiesced in the way of the world), the first thing which a wise man must learn in order to retain his own good opinion is not to mistake his prejudices for his convictions, or *vice versa*. When he has learned this lesson he must expect to enjoy some isolation, for in retaining his own good opinion in this way he must forfeit that of others. But then a fine, amusing prejudice can flourish much more hardily independent of sympathy than with it. A good, harmless prejudice for a man who needs some intellectual distraction, and is not naturally vicious, is a prejudice against critics. It is perhaps, indeed, due simply to the universality of this prejudice among authors that the critics are read at all. There are prejudices of greater moment, but scarcely one that affords more constant amusement. And with these vague hints I must close, for, unfortunately, there is a growing prejudice against long sermons.

JACOBITISM IN BOSTON.

I.

One of the most quotation-worn of Matthew Arnold's oft-quoted dicta, is the declaration that "poetry is at bottom a criticism of life;" and, accepting for a moment this profound judgment in something of that superficial aspect in which we have been made familiar with it in cocksure critical paragraphing, we link it to a commonplace when we say that the commonest poetic criticism of our time is that it is wofully degenerate and prosaic. This is not only the poetic criticism of our time, but is also the everyday commonplace echo and haphazard complacent verdict of every tea table.

But in referring to poetic criticism let us be precise. This is the criticism of the few poets (among the great multitude of literary lice, that lie snugly and fatten in

the public ear and repeat in sugared flatteries the vaporings of the public's too
many mouths), who see both true poetry
and true criticism trampled into the dust,
in order that the hard-earned coins may be
cozened out of the pockets of poor boozy
and bamboozled King Demos; and this
judgment is expressed not so often in print,
in either poetry or prose, as in the ebb and
flow of talk in a club or tavern corner, or
in a garret with a few volumes of the old
true poets; for it is characteristic of our
glorious contemporary literature that all
opinion must perforce coincide with public
opinion. The inevitable result of this
preposterous law is that all honest opinion
is either *private* opinion, or it raises its
wicked fangs in such deep obscurity that
even the Archangel Michael is not likely
to remark the flash in the darkness.

And let us note, in a by the way, before
passing on, that this dictum of Matthew
Arnold's, this fine philosophic compendium
in a phrase, is, like all such phrases, in
danger of becoming hackneyed as a phrase
without its deep and true meaning being
apprehended. Indeed, the very careless-
ness with which it can be thrown about in

hasty reviewing and in club corner scrap-
bag talk, is enough to debar its true ring
of spiritual truth from debasing the common currency. We have just exemplified
with what a fine relevancy it can be mar-
ried to an irrelevancy.

But to return. It is certain that, from
the poetic standpoint, the very commonplace of criticism is that our modern life
is lacking in color, is destitute of contrast
and variety, is desperately drab, is irritat-
ingly ugly and is so hideously probable.
We have almost robbed Death itself of its
holy and beautiful mystery, its grandeur
and dignity, its solemn and divine re-
minders and promptings, thronging thick
and fast into heart and brain at its very
name, by making it the daily theme and
vulgar commodity of our unclean and
malodorous newspapers. In the bloodiest
eras of antiquity and of the mediæval ages,
when fire and sword, pillage and violence
and rapine were so common, life itself was
cheap enough, but death was the grand
mystery; and bloodthirsty, gory heroes
would no more gibe at the dead than, in
their revels, they would toast their gods as
they would a wanton. In all their rude-

ness there was enough of superstition to keep them from becoming unqualified brutes.

In our age superstition, except in political affairs and literature, has largely disappeared, and with it many wholesome restraints. There is now no respect for heroes, alive or dead; and life is certainly held as cheap as ever. Who cares how many poor serfs perish every winter of cold and hunger because good Mr. Dives has shut down his mills and has gone to bring his daughter out in London society? And as for the mystery of death, is it not only the opportunity of the jackals and vultures of the Press to emerge from their holes to gorge themselves and make unclean noises? At every street corner poor pigmy dealers in blood and woe and every sort of moral grime rustle their enticing wares under our eyes, and with chill penury in their poor, hungry, hoarse and earnest voices, they tempt us with their foul odors and scraps of ghoulish bait. We say we cannot live without *the news*. We devour every scrap of horror to sate our contempt of our kind; and then we subscribe to send missionaries to the Can-

nibal Islands ! It is indeed terribly fitting
that such histories of horror should have
such poor tragic little brokers to hawk them
in our streets. Another age saw the slaugh-
ter of the Innocents. It has been reserved
for this Christian time, and the civilization
of this Western world, so prolific of fine
charities in bricks and stones, to publicly
abandon the Innocents to the Devil, to
pipe his wares at all hours of the day and
night, in the most tragical and villainous
of childish trebles that ever ears and hearts
listened to.

Our modern life is indeed horribly probable, and realistic enough to satisfy the
most desperate and perverted glutton of
facts. In America especially, Gradgrind
is the undisputed Titan of the hour. After
centuries of labor he is thrown out of the
womb of old Time as the finished product
of civilization, and he makes God's world
a great hell in which the naked spin to
clothe the drones, and the starvelings
slave to feed the sated. It may shock a
great many serious-minded, severe, and
comfortable good souls, but I suspect the
Devil emulates them in their lively passion
for facts !

But still I cannot quite bring myself to subscribe, without some mental reservation, to this altogether sceptical view of the poetic materials afforded by even the ugliness of our modern life; for I think there is often some serious defect in our vision and in our sympathies. The stuff upon the ".roaring loom of Time" can never, we must dare assert, become wholly uninteresting or wholly drab in any generation; and then, too, the tragedy of drab is not, we may be quite positive, as yet at all fully understood. So I think our criticism is more rational, even confining ourselves to the immediate aspect of the matter, and not taking the whole purview of the nature and elements of literature, when we look for the causes of any passing eclipse of poetry, in those harsh circumstances and' arbitrary conditions of social and governmental systems, which create false ideals, subdue and obscure the beauty and sublimity of human life and nature, and shackle and poison the imagination. Only a very strong, great and original spirit can endure outlawry; and with the strongest, the only safeguard against self-sacrifice often is that some idiosyncracy of tempera-

ment cheats intention, and makes conformity physically impossible, even in those
moments when the moral force is fretted
away, and the will itself condemns resolution as rash egoism.   And in our day and
generation, as in others before it, a great
poet must perforce live as an outcast, a
wretched villifier of the high and sublime
smugness and complacency of Philistinism.
    The trouble with many of our poets
seems to be that they are too much dependent upon our beguiling, marring sympathy; they are much too cognizant and
commiserate of our spiritual deficiencies.
A great poet must write as if his generation was a race of archangels — which
Heaven knows no race of men has ever
been!   But that is the standard.   Our
poets — the majority of those who have
broken cover — know our small ken only
too well.   They drink tea with us and
read "poems of occasion" at political dinners and church sociables.   They have
altogether too much consanguinity with us.
They live too near us out of the spirit, and
to our small preoccupations, to see
the spectacle of human life in our day (the
old, old phantasmagoria,) in its true pro-

portions, and so, while they are well fitted
to serve us, as they do with more or less
pertinence and diffidence, in the capacity
of optimistic clowns or Job's comforters,
they cannot put new color and spiritual
grace into our busily barren lives.

But although this commends itself to my
imagination as a seeming philosophic view
of the matter, we must not wantonly
weaken the truth in a general opinion, or
we may forfeit a wholesome and large view
(which may quicken reformative influences),
to dodge around noisome alley-ways after
shadows — shadows which prove only too
often to be the shadows of corpses. The
spirit of toleration is, of course, desirable;
but while it may touch charity, it must stop
short of its precipitate and undignified
exaggerations, or all imagination is dissipated in the endeavor to prove its existence
in all manner of small parcels of bald fact.
Then the mind loses that elasticity, which
in the rebound makes any and every moral
hope possible. Promiscuous charity in
intellectual affairs, as promiscuous love in
the affairs of the heart, makes us poor
indeed without enriching a single soul; it
leaves us bankrupt in enthusiasm and in

friends. Carried to this excess, swept away from our moorings in this timorous passion for exactitude, our liberalism too often becomes mere latitude, our cherished facts mere fantasy, and our good nature and patience simply indifference. If one is ambitious to live and die without a single friend, one should turn away from one's familiar friends to court all the world's favorites. There are so many good people so "broad" that they are too broad for tolerance, and too narrow to experience a holy human indignation. For these, right and wrong lose their geography — every thing is a happy chaos; and, comfortably sitting upon the brink, they placidly fold their hands over it all, having parcelled out their difficulties among the different clubs and societies which are organized to dispose of such things — and tea.

And yet it would be a waste of charity to let it stand here, that these worthy folk in devising a common conscience for their individual apathies, are content to deprive themselves of all interest in that which may happen to lie beyond the range of their sympathies and understanding; for, on the contrary, with "rubbing the poor itch of their opinion" they do "make themselves scabs."

It is therefore simply a desire to prove how I shrink from these treacherous dallyings of sympathy, to establish the fact of my orthodoxy (in spite of this catholic and dubious discursiveness), which leads me to declare there is sufficient truth in this general indictment of the ignoble strife of our perpetual market-day civilization, the evidence so far satisfies my scruples of conscience, and so strongly supports the conclusion of *drab*, that if I were upon the Bench to find a verdict, without the dull wits of a jury to stop the course of justice, to hang or acquit my generation of villainous commonplaceness, I am sorely afraid my generation would hang.

But it would be difficult indeed to find a jury of good and reputable, or even disreputable, citizens with enough appreciation of poetic justice among them to consider the evidence and arguments in this weighty matter in the necessary spirit of proxy humility. I am afraid the counsel for the prosecution would have to challenge every mother's son who might be summoned. We may be quite sure that proper humility

would be out of the question with our poor
human nature. Possibly twelve members
of the Suicide Club could be found to
bring enough philosophy to bear upon the
matter to serve as jurymen; but even in
such fortune we could scarcely hope to
elude the vile and detestable prejudices of
the defence. Commonplace people, whatever may be their virtues — and they sometimes possess an uncomfortable quantity of
them, although seldom much variety — are
not usually endowed with even the most
embryonic humility; and they always
regard people with ideals, who suffer in
the constant collision with ugliness, which
usually rides over them rough-shod, as pit-
iably airy creatures. On the other hand,
those who have some sense of beauty and
the relative values of the things of life and
are possessed by a desire of some ideal fulfillment in life of their o'er fond dreaming,
not only carry the burden of their own
tragedy, but they make themselves miserable over the tragic show of the commonplace in the everyday world, — in which by
the way, presumably to cure them of such
misanthropic humors, they are often cast
for motley. One would like to prescribe a

course of Plato to the Furies — but they are doubtless too busy to get any philosophy, and so we have no refuge from their wicked whimsies. The idealists are doubtless right in regarding the commonplace as tragic. It is; but it is dismally ludicrous also.

This gravity is the gravest error of judgment of the idealists, for, since human society is constituted as it is, with its heels in the air, our only possible serenity in life is in our point of view; and to be happy in this world, whose beauty is marred by the ugly ideas it contains, one must learn to regard the ugly as ludicrous. Herein lies the one compensation for those whose vision and morals are not hopelessly tangled.

It must be admitted, however, that this is a sort of stoicism for which Nature does not fit all whom she intends for high purposes. A too vivid perception of the ludicrous is often, in times of distress, a lure to that entire philosophic resignation which easily becomes apathy; and so Dame Nature denies a sense of humor to many fine and noble spirits. And, it must be confessed, that it is hard to make a gibe of a life of moral crucifixion; and when this Mark Tapleyan temperament is lacking, it is impossible to laugh content into ears that sorrow has dulled to all such jocund Jesuitry.

I think in this dropsical prolegomenon, I have at least shown that it is by no means easy to make-believe, when we are quite grown up, in this materialistic time. We ought therefore to be exceeding grateful to any persons who are courageous enough to cherish some utterly unpractical ideals, to dream some beautiful, tender dreams, and to find in the ribald irreverence and incredulousness of the most hopelessly contemporary of their contemporaries, but a fresh impulse to a martyrdom of consoling reflections. Any persons who dare to put a bit of color into our desperately "practical," "utility" lives should obtain our respect, since we are most of us afraid to cut any capers of our own ; although it must be said, with entire relevance, that the volume of original sin in the world has certainly not diminished, and we stumble through the decalogue quite as often as did our forefathers in a larger day.

And perhaps, after all, we are not so grim as our occupations and our transgressions would seem to suggest. There are perhaps many of us who would gladly caper a little now and then, but we are disconcerted to find upon the hazard that, while one talent may be sufficient to cut a very respectable figure in the world in any serious calling, for exquisite fooling a man can have all the talents given to mortals, — and then fail.

It would, of course, be invidious to put into cold print the cause of such failures: and the good people who are rash enough to leave their native atmosphere and creep for awhile into this bleakness, have usually too much mercy upon themselves to carry their accidental discoveries to disagreeable conclusions.

But, although all our wonderment is expected nowadays to spin round the big driving wheels of gigantic machinery, there are still some poor benighted souls in the world in whose minds the buzz and whir of all this wonderful machinery awakens no reverential mood, to whom it is buzz and whir and no more, and who shamelessly cling to unprofitable and antiquated

ideals merely to understand certain mad
poets and other thinking riff-raff. " Poor,
pathetic creatures ! " we may say of such
men, with our fine practicality, our good
common-sense interest in dividends, and
our touchingly pathetic belief in an
impending millennium of dynamos and
driving wheels, when all the world will
make holiday and none will lack bread for
lack of work.

Since, however, none who draw fat dividends care a stiver for this millennium, let us
reconsider the moral condition of these perverted dreamers, who are so unfortunate as
to be out of sympathy with the social dog-
mas of their day. When we have had
pleasant dreams it is always something of a
shock to awake to reality. But what if we
could wake into a world of dreams as real ?
This, of course, is a privilege accorded to few.
But these poor, pitiable, deluded wretches
at any rate cherish the most delicious of
mocking dreams, that are far more satisfactory than those exaggerated professions
which bind them together, and by which they
are judged of men ; and they meet in the
flesh and talk of a fine fantastical world,
which never was, and never will be, possible

in this world, and they read beautiful and
whimsical books — and sometimes write
them! We should therefore occasionally
permit ourselves to taste the joys of a reckless immoral magnanimity, and thank
Heaven that the monotonous drab of our
day is relieved here and there with a few
patches of such fine old glowing revolutionary Toryism — for it is the Tory who is the
revolutionary in our society.

This is precisely the admirable and
delightful utility of the Jacobites, who, perhaps largely on account of the wholly
unpractical and sentimental character of
the society, are in force in this picturesque
old Puritan city of Boston.

II.

THE Jacobite society exists in Boston as
the actual embodiment in the intellectual
life of the city of certain social and æsthetic ideas, which are so preposterously
antiquated and impossible in this age as to
cause an inquiring mind to hesitate before
putting them aside as familiar and worthless, or merely curious. They are so antiquated as to suggest the shadow of the
"latest" fashion, and they are so evidently

exaggerated as to arouse a suspicion of smugglery. It is one of the interesting and remarkable contradictions of the human mind, that, while it most often uses the appearance of ingenuousness and sincerity to achieve selfish ends, it sometimes uses the garb of avowed insincerity to conceal some prohibited and banned sincere and honest, noble thought and purpose.

One should remember Shakespeare's fools and study well the judgments of motley. Perchance in their uncurbed, fantastical similitudes, we may stumble upon motley where before we saw but sober justice; discover mere players' passion where we thought was a Man voicing the tragedy of the world, and, this is most common, find only a pinchbeck mask of gravity where we thought was wisdom and philosophy. This habit of cautious curiosity is one of the advantages to be derived from some desultory reading. Every lover of books has learned to know that the moonlight dreams of one age have become the veriest commonplaces of another. There is a good family of perfectly sane ideas in the silent world of books that are obscured for the reader of violent prejudice in the

intentional grotesqueness and exaggeration in which they have been enveloped, so
that they might steal into the world, and,
in a twinkling, snatch the festal robes and
cerements from the bodies of old delusions
without immediate detection. Such viola-
tion is often discovered by a few discerning ones the moment it is committed. But
the force of the ridiculous is both so strong
and so subtle, that even gravity sometimes
forgives sacrilege in the guise of motley;
and absolves its tender public conscience
at the instigation of its imputative private
ditto, with the consoling reflection, that
there is already almost enough wisdom
between covers in the libraries to cure half
the world's ills, but none of it will ever get
into the heads of the masses. The worldly
wise in the quick in every generation will
see to it that the masses do not neglect
their own magic piping for the unbending
wisdom of the sages. This is the reason
why the most passionate poet of the right
finds his warmest adherents and closest
students among those who have a vested
interest in wrong. They have, from the
force of contrast, an intense intellectual
curiosity about that which their interest

forbids them to know through experience; and so, paradoxically, the greatest poets and thinkers, who naturally take the broadest and sanest views of life, appeal most strongly to the few, who would suffer material loss if their enthusiasm for the right ever struggled out of the region of intellectual abstraction. In this matter of the philosophy of misery we all have an intense scorn of empiricists and show an unconquerable attachment to transcendentalism. The multitude, by the same law of the attraction of opposites, have an absorbing interest in the glitter and glamour of supercilious injustice and wrong; and their poets are aliens among them.

As I suspected upon my first acquaintance with the Jacobite society, the organic idea of the constitution and by-laws is the least significant thing about the movement. It is perhaps the one question under heaven most infrequently discussed at the meetings of the society. The constitution serves the admirable purpose, not wholly foreign to other weighty societies, of bringing the members together at regular intervals to discuss matters more or less irrelevant to the objects of the league. Indeed, one of the most delightful circumstances of membership in this society, is, that one is never under any sort of obligation to say anything at all relevant to the avowed purposes of the constitution.

But on the other hand, the Jacobite society in Boston is only properly understood when one allows proper significance to its perfectly irrelevant interests, and accepts the constitution as mere literature. Just as about all the actual democracy in the United States was squeezed once for all into the magnificent periods of Jefferson's famous declaration, so all the principles of the Jacobite league are mirrored in its constitution — where they are beautiful and innocuous. This constitution, by the way, is not sufficiently esteemed by the Jacobites themselves. It is as stuffed full of plums as a haggis. It is quite as sober as *Punch*, but it is filled with the tenable contradictions of all possible ideas, and is so deliciously ridiculous in its gravity. I have always been curious to learn who inspired this document, for it is the work of many hands; but the mystery, like that of the authorship of the beautiful English of the Book of Common Prayer, is unsolvable.

It is, of course, as well that this mystery should exist. For the testament of any great movement should not be traceable to any one author, so that envious criticism and bigotry can lay violent hands upon an individual and so gibbet with its author both gospel and gospellers.

Unsuspected, or almost unsuspected, Jacobites, are to be found in all the ramifications of our society. It may be they exist in other cities on this side of the Atlantic, but I doubt if Jacobitism could find so congenial an atmosphere in any other American city as it finds in Boston. The comfortable classes here were just ripe for Jacobitism — or any other fine crusade that was unreal and impossible enough. Its progress in Boston among the fortunates who have leisure enough to think, has been remarkable, and ought to convince the most sceptical. It is hard in this materialistic time to find any refuge for the weary spirit, buffeted at every turn by the highly objectionable gospellers of fact and so-called "progress," so that the success of the Jacobite movement in Boston is distinctly encouraging to all those optimists, who, in divorcing hope, want enough elbow-room in their own day to make merry and thank the good God. There are plenty of modern gospels which insure martyrdom in a very real and vulgar life of pinching poverty, but this is perhaps the most attractive of all the reform move- ments, that call forth one's most earnest and serious sympathy, without in the least impinging one's sacred identity in a career of highly respectable wrong-doing. In my own case, I do not mind confessing that my sympathies were never so entirely and unreservedly enlisted in any other cause, however worthy, as they have been in Jacobitism; and the reason is, doubtless, that its promoters acknowledge that it is absolutely chimerical.

But the Jacobites have the courage of their convictions, both moral and immoral, and they are not timorous in the expres- sion of their ideas. They do not care for that great bugaboo of democracy, Public Opinion, and they dare to rail openly upon the ugliness of our civilization and prog- ress. Therefore to veil private spleen I am a good Jacobite. It is eminently enjoyable to dignify private distresses into public catastrophes.

It is not every idealistic propaganda in this ugly and materialistic time, which is sufficiently impossible to .tempt the discerning and discreet into martyrdom. One has to be careful to make proper investigation into these various reform movements before one embarks; even when they have doctors of divinity on the committees. And, by the way, doctors of divinity are usually so desperately afraid of being suspected of even the least tiptoeing on the solid earth, that one almost suspects they are more fearful of their deacons than they are of their consciences or their divinity. But D. D.'s are so often D. F.'s that one has to be cautious, even in following them, if one would enjoy the pleasures of martyrdom without incurring any of its penalties.

There are so many reforms, which are like the evils for which they are prescribed as antidotes, like in one fatal circumstance — they are but too possible, too obvious. These are the movements a wise man will shun; they involve a loss of social prestige, and an infinitude of sacrifices and embarrassments. They are not sufficiently remote to satisfy the really fine spirit, that is naturally ambitious of a martyrdom of opinion, but also shrinks from the idea of any vulgar collision with distressing facts, whose only remedy in the large tolerant Christian mind is *forgetfulness.*

Now here is a really excellent and tenable argument, quite by the way, for it has only just occurred to me, for the paunchy and frothy comfortable ones in our pulpits. The cure for love, it is the wisdom of all ages and sages, is love, and when that is not to be encompassed, forgetfulness. And therefore if one is so unfortunate as to feel a preposterous concern in the woes and miseries of humanity at large, if one loves one's neighbor as one's self, the proper cure is, logically enough, *forgetfulness.* It needs no argument to prove, to even the most illiberal mind, that it is impossible to forget *one's self;* and since to carry the woes of others is but to add a new misery to the burden of misery already existing in the world, and since it is perfectly possible to put one's neighbors' woes out of one's mind, it is the duty of every man who has the happiness of mankind at heart, to diminish unnecessary misery by forgetting his neighbors' troubles as quickly as they arise. This habit once formed, one soon attains perfection, and in a very little while ceases to be cognizant of the existence of any evils, except those that cross one's own threshold. This is perhaps the only thing in which perfection is granted to poor human endeavor; but precept and practice need never be divorced in this code of morality.

I rather think that this bit of logic solves one of the prime difficulties of the disparity between the Christian credo and Christian conduct to a nicety; and moreover, with an éclat of morality, which, I regret to say, is too often sadly lacking in the apologies of many ecclesiastics of most exalted station. I sometimes sigh when I think what a fine mystical theologian was lost to the world when I was dragged down by my necessities into the noisome obscurity of literary brigandage.

But if we admit every happy thought, our budget will become too bulky.

The prosperity which has attended the Jacobite movement, shows beyond all dispute that the magic of the old name has not entirely departed. There are hundreds of good comfortable souls, brought up in a strictly Puritanical moral atmosphere (a euphemism for the most incurable sort of immorality, by the way), to regard the very word "reform" as a dangerous plague spot in the lexicon, who have rushed incontinently into this revolutionary propaganda of obscurantism, without the least comprehension of its incidental reactionary purposes — which happen to be the only ones that the leaders of the movement are ever suspected of being at all soberly interested in.

It may appear incredible but I am assured by some of the Jacobite leaders, men very high in office, that not only are there serious men in the society, but there are actually *serious Jacobites*. It is all very well to be a mild Jacobin in our plutocratic society, although one must be more careful in declaring Jacobinism, than one need to be in avowing Jacobitism; but a sober, serious Jacobite is a sorry spectacle, for the Jacobites are indeed belated. Of course, in a certain way, the Jacobites here are really Jacobins, but, from inherited prejudices, they abhor and despise the label; and it certainly is involved in odious traditions about which time can throw no kindly glamour. But the Jacobins can be taken quite soberly when discovered, for despite their evil traditions, they comprise today the thinking, submerged minority that is disloyal to the superstitions of both monarchy and democracy, in order to be loyal to truth, to posterity, and to God.

I have only seen one serious Jacobite, and he almost caused my sentimental gravity to collapse. There are certain precautions necessary to the preservation of this gravity (and of course politeness is one of the cardinal virtues in Jacobite society, as it should be everywhere), which are absolutely essential to obtaining the quintessence of ludicrousness out of the delightful debates in Jacobite gatherings.

It is easy to understand that one cannot get all the humor out of any situation, when one chills the sobriety of the actors with inopportune, or too opportune, wintry jesting. I cannot describe all the necessary precautions here, since I intend to confine myself principally to the more important, incidental interests of Jacobitism — which shows what an incurably serious minded person I am, in spite of my hypocrisy of Jacobitish sympathies. A

truly frivolous-minded writer would concern himself wholly with the fundamental
principles of the movement. But I may
mention one circumstance. I am writing
this paper in broad daylight, in one of the
back rooms of a city boarding-house, and
the windows look out upon a dreary vista of
city yards, and back windows, and murky
clean clothes, and ash barrels, ragged
children, and forlorn, peripatetic cats, and
old "clo'" and bottle merchants — a desperately dreary, untidy and uncompromis-
ingly realistic world. I cannot see all this
at present, but I *have* seen it from a hund-
red back windows, and the mention of it
makes my pen pause in mid-air, for the
unmitigable ugliness of it all is borne in
upon my mind; and that is fatal to gravity,
though not to sorrow and heart-aches.
Outside, too, I know, is the sunshine and
the blue vault of heaven, flecked with
golden clouds; but these only intensify
those realistic and democratic back yards,
and so the shutters are drawn and closed
tight, the thick winter curtains make a solemn midnight of the day, and tall, spectral
candles throw an uncertain, fantastic light,
in which I can gravely believe in almost

any fantasy, even in divine rights, even in humanity, and the provable existence of the Golden Rule.

The small heresies of discretion are the traitors to every great cause, and they proclaim the mere merchant in the soldier, the priest, poet or philosopher; for, unfortunately, this is a world in which everything is taken to market, even thought. But man, possibly because he is the only created being capable of laughter, is violently in love with the judicial character. A man cannot be a hero in either action or thought who is fearful of laughter. It is easy to defy the wrath of the wise, and thrive upon opposition, but the laughter of fools has destroyed sages and heroes. A man who shows himself impervious to popular opinion and cat-calls is at least worthy of our respect. The Jacobites are not, therefore, to be put too lightly aside, for they are possessed of that robust self-sufficiency which can repay laughter with laughter. Hence the necessity of a man's earnestly believing in his hobby, if he would enjoy life and play his part with dignity in an isolation of his own high approbation.

And, thank Heaven! there is nothing too impossible and fantastic, but that someone can find a belief in it the one satisfaction of life. It must indeed be a desperately possible crusade for which an earnest, persistent prophet cannot find good, trusty henchmen. But to seek proselytes for a perfectly hopeless cause is the delightfullest occupation of gravity. To be hailed everywhere as an apostle of paradox, the revealer of impossible truths, whose audacity is quite innocent, because too hopelessly divorced from convincing platitudes (the very bed-and-board realities of all great political games), is to pass one's days in a delicious dream of martyrdom.

I have been all my life long too fatally apt to discern the fact, that no parties are all good or all bad, to be able to expect much preferment or pudding or gratitude at the hands of any partisans; and I am troubled with an uneasy consciousness of the probability of an impeachment at the bar at the next meeting of the Jacobite league, for the small indiscretions of discretion I have committed in this paper. It goes hard with any man in this world who pleads the cause of the opposition in ⸗

whatever camp he may be; but to arrive at
even proximate truth this is precisely what
a man of integrity must do. Most men
fall so easily into parties, because there is
a popular superstition, that, while corpor-
ations have no souls, there is a sort of aggre-
gate conscience in parties; and this, with
the support of the popular suffrage behind
it, by a process of metaphysics I cannot
pretend to follow, absolves the individual
conscience for the abandonment of the
trouble of examination and continual vigi-
lance, and the worry of decisions. It is
this indolence, which makes parties practicable, by creating a popular opinion
that may, with some sort of security, be
relied upon. If all men weighed every
question and thought for themselves, all
parties would serve but their temporary purposes, and then become dissipated into new
combinations of opinion. But as no two
prophets think alike, parties have their
usefulness.

There are men, and unfortunately I am
one of them, on the other hand, who never
attain to any of the dignities of life,
because they cannot keep their hands off
the dignitaries. It may be scarcely cred-

ited by those of my readers who have so often seen me play the ghost of poor Yorick, but I have been all my life long a Puritan — a Puritan in love with Jacobite ideals and with uncorrupted, philosophical Jacobinism; and, as may be imagined, in a devil of a quandary, with my conscience first in one camp and then in the other, and my cause without a friend in either. However, if I have not had that advancement and emolument that lies along the path of orthodoxy, I have had, in a career of transformations, almost as many lives as a cat — and that is some compensation!

If I have written with some freedom of the relative importance of the principles of Jacobitism, I have done so because to exaggerate their importance would be to diminish the beneficial influences of the active concerns of the Jacobites in the region of art and literature, and in the encouragement of the toleration of tolerance. Causes which have only certain invisible ends to serve, and not facts to reveal, are best served by partisan hirelings, who will only see one side of a fence, unless they hear of bigger pay on the other side, and then they will crawl under. But, fortunately, the Jacobite cause is sufficiently impossible to allow of one playing the traitor without treason, and bribery and corruption is luckily out of the question. Of course, if there was the ghost of a chance of a Jacobite revolt and restoration, and the prospect of a seat upon the woolsack in return for my valuable missionary services, I should not perhaps be quite so prepared to don and doff respect and allegiance upon the reading of every other clause in the constitution, simply to preserve the judicial character and the approbation of my own conscience.

But with the unpolitical Jacobin portion of the programme, respecting the introduction into this country of intellectual and moral freedom in the shaping of the arts, so completely dominated in our day by alien influences, I am in entire and earnest sober sympathy. The vulgarization of literature as merchandise, made to tickle fools, is complete in our day. It certainly encourages the good *gens gris* of letters, who sell words as they would playing cards, and whose opinions (unlike the cards, which do teach the prosperous certain lessons in the even-handedness of

Chance) take the color of every bidder's gold; but it outlaws all thinkers, who recognize the sanctity of words. We must be far gone indeed in this barbarism of supply and demand, when men, and men who have had every advantage of education, of communion with the greatest minds of all times in their collegiate course, with a knowledge of the mystic grandeur surrounding the creation and evolution of human language, can talk glibly, and smile, of selling *mere words.* There are no such things as mere words,— except in the dictionaries. Once marshal words in any array and they are good or evil existences. Thoughts and words are sacred things. Those of us who have been born in the outer darkness of poverty, who have had to struggle upward under bitter burdens to gain the mouth of the pit, before we could begin to climb to the height where we could understand the thoughts of the world's great men, who have had to buy with sweat and blood the right to think our own thoughts, and find our own souls, know there are no *mere words!* This is largely the bane of good, prosperous mediocrity, which inherits its ideas of the uses of knowledge in the same way that it does its houses and lands and furniture, and in colleges and in society it finds that the teachings of the wise are not considered *realities*, but only intellectual exercises, bundles of beautiful words, foot-balls, to kick about for sport, matters entirely irrelevant in the actual world. With men bred in this thick atmosphere our contemporary literature is filled. It is astonishing we should have so many Universities in America and so few *real* men, so little *real* literature, so little *real* knowledge of the true nature and offices of knowledge. Wherever — let us out with this bit of sober heresy! — wherever there is a true man that stands up before all the world and proclaims the absolute reality and grandeur of *thought*, there is a university whose degrees are worth winning.

I join heart and soul in all the vigorous protests of Jacobitism against the odious moral slavery of our cramped, smug, vulgar, ludicrous nursery art. With this heretical nonsense about the necessity, for gradual educative purposes (sic!), of dragging all thought down to the vacuous pruriency of the vulgar, completely dominant in our art and in our criticism, with our art ever crawling on all fours to carry the heaven-sent middleman on its back, and to make sport for Dives' too corruptible babes and maids, we must thank God for the advent of Jacobitism. How are these babes and maids ever to learn to put away childish things and understand the real world about them with such instruction?

It seems a little hard to an audacious imagination, that a literature for grown-up men and women should not be permitted in our noble, flexible, virile English tongue, so equipped for all the purposes of great Titanic imaginings. Why, since youth is such a fleeting period, and life really begins with the passions of maturity, why should there be no literature in our time for the mature? We have to hie back to our English classics to touch the thoughts of *men*. To read one's contemporaries in the department of imaginative literature, in this country at least, is almost tantamount to sentencing one's mind to a lifetime of the sucking-bottle. Mrs. Grundy reigns supreme in America, and many fine imaginations she whips into poor popular drivellers. But the Muse is sometimes unconjugal, and kicks over the traces —

and then we get the Jacobites in art, the jovial outlaws, who outlaw the whole critical Bench, and delight all the sweet chicks under Mrs. Grundy's wing. Their primal consciousness of art does not begin with the catechism and the social decalogue. The only superstitions they allow as valid are those of art. In so far as Jacobitism is educative in this direction, I hope I may never be found compounding with the Philistines, even for a bishopric.

III.

To all those hideously practical folk who may object that these things do not constitute any tangible aim and purpose for an association of men, I beg leave to say, that the Jacobites are educating the miserable progeny of poor Plutus, born under a stifling cloud of gold-dust, to be something more than merely rich, to be interested in something finer and nobler and more real than the mere breeding of money, and they have put some color into the monotonous drab of our buying and selling society. That is something. It is, at any rate, as good a reason for any human association as that of many solemn societies, in which men meet to exchange toasts and make vapid speeches about trade, progress, political morality, and other abstractions, with nothing improbable about the whole affair, except perhaps intoxication. Our age has grown so decorous over its wine that even its Joe Millers are imbued with a bit of cant. We pass all our days under the ban of respectability, and while it is held to be iniquitous to express an original idea, it is infamous and eccentric to imitate the wise. But to dissent from the opinions of high authority and gravity, which are not kin to the wise, is to invite social ostracism. It is easy to win the golden opinions of the elect, if one will only combine with the judicial character that fine optimism that jostles humanity, pity, and justice out of court. It is the penalty of mere success in a democracy that it is only to be attained through the imitation of solemn fools and poseurs. The ideals of a supply and demand democracy can never rise above the flood-tide of respectability.

I am under bonds not to reveal the place of meeting where we toast Prince Charlie "over the sea." In the present

edition of the interesting Stuart family, to
be strictly accurate, it is Prince Robert of
Bavaria. At these Jacobite meetings, it is
interesting to note we drink in the good
old Jacobite exile fashion — across, and not
out of, the water bottle; and I think this
would please even such a stout Hanoverian as old Dr. Johnson himself, with his
fine Homeric declaration for tippling:
"Claret for boys, port for men, and brandy
for Heroes" — and his beautiful allegiance to Bohea! If you are old-fashioned
enough in your ideas to enjoy a rollicking
good time, without the formalities of the
ordinary dinner party, but with certain
modern æsthetic exaggerations and mod-
ifications, I should enjoin Jacobitism.

I have always been somewhat deficient
in history, and have been a Jacobite
rather from moral conviction than evidence, as I have been a Puritan more from
evidence than conviction, so that when I
sat down to write this paper I found I had
not sufficient historical data, and writing
away from books, I was obliged to have
recourse to my good friend Napier
McDougall, the laird of Highdudgeon
Peak, one of the most prominent and most

picturesque of the Jacobite leaders in Boston, for a precise exposition of the political principles and hopes of Jacobitism. This, of course, was very bitter; but it saved much laborious reading and time, and also obviated all danger of my drifting into wild conjectures; and I am an authority upon the historical aspects of Jacobitism from this day forth. About all I actually knew of the hopes and standing of the cause in these latter days, I am free to confess, was that the old Pretender was as dead as Queen Anne.

According to the views of my friend, however, the sympathies of the American colonies were largely with the House of Stuart from the beginning of the Parliamentary struggle in England, and the principles of the Parliamentarians never did have any strong hold upon the imaginations of the exiles for conscience' sake on this side of the Atlantic. In support of this view there is the fact that the first charter of the Massachusetts Bay Colony was issued under the hand and seal of Charles I. That is strong enough logic for any good sentimental Jacobite.

The Jacobites believe that history has

been largely wrongly written; and it is scarcely necessary to believe in Jacobitism to quite concur in this view. What Oscar Wilde says of "Debrett's Peerage," we can say of half the English histories—that they are "the best things in fiction the English have ever done."

There is the American Revolution, of course—but the Jacobites find no difficulty in dealing with this matter. With a largeness of view, which it would be a good thing for most self-satisfied democrats and others, even enthusiastic moral Jacobins, to emulate in this and other matters, they declare it is perfectly possible for an American to believe in the principles of the Revolution, and to believe in them ardently, and yet at the same time uphold the ideals of Jacobitism. The war was not against England, but against the vile Hanoverian who occupied the throne of England, and it was because of his oppressions that the outraged colonists revolted. They had no ill-feeling against the Crown as an institution, or against monarchy as a system of Government; and there is a tradition, which the Jacobites acknowledge as a tradition, but are naturally loth to part with, that after the Declaration of Independence, there was a movement on foot among the leaders and substantial men of the victorious revolutionaries to invite the Chevalier de St. George, commonly known as the "Old Pretender," to take the throne in America. But the Prince was old and broken down, and the project fell through.

And there is another more or less authenticated story, which the Jacobites do not forget to recite in this connection, to the effect that the crown was then offered to George Washington, who, as is well known, declined the honor. The Jacobites claim that Washington, realizing he had no divine right to the regal character, put aside the ambition of his friends, because he feared the embroilments of factions and rivalries and violence such as rent Rome under the Cæsars.

The more moderate of the Jacobites, who have an ambition to make their sentimental diversion serve some useful purpose in the dignifying of popular opinion and taste, content themselves with pointing out that the master minds of the Revolution, Washington, the Adamses,

Franklin, Jefferson, Hamilton, and the rest, all belonged to the aristocracy of intellect and fine spirit; and none could be more shocked than they if they were to return to earth and witness the vulgar excesses and the depravity of modern plutocracy, in politics, in journalism and in literature. They none of them believed in the whims of the lowest being gratified at the cost and sacrifice of the interests of the highest. Napier McDougall, the laird of Highdudgeon, believes that even Sam Adams, the most democratic of them all, would rather have paid the tax on tea and said no more about it, if the alternative had been presented of his days being prolonged to our time with the necessity of reading the enormities of our Sunday newspapers. As for Dr. Franklin and Alexander Hamilton, those two splendid figures in history, who raised dignity to a fine art, we certainly cannot doubt for a moment what would be their opinion of the prostitution of the printing-press and the labors and thoughts of the study in the interests of plutocracy to exploit the poor, benighted hoodlums of the democracy.

The Revolution was not undertaken by

the fathers of the Republic to establish a
democracy of darkness, but to remedy certain outrages that infringed on the dignity
of the commonwealth.   Unfortunately it is
much easier to overthrow a monarchy or
an autocracy than it is to render a democracy tolerable to pass one's life in.

But to show that we are not incapable
of seeing both sides of a question, let us
anticipate the criticism of the regnant
powers, and quote the snort of unshak-
able respectabilism—" *That* is all mere
fustian!" But, ah! the irony of Time's
revenges, to think that Toryism and Sans-
culottism should so change places, that
Toryism should have to storm in impo-
tence against the iron rule of its old
contempt!

In the abstract, the Jacobite idea of
government is based upon the idea that
the power of kingship comes from above
and not from the consent of the governed.
This is in the Jacobite constitution.   The
sentimental gravity I maintain, when I
hear it read in solemn convocation, is, I
am convinced, excellent discipline for me.
The Jacobites think that the Stuarts are
the best representatives of the old idea of

kingship, as opposed to what they call the debased and circumscribed kingship of the Hanoverians; and they sincerely sympathize with the unfortunate condition which has obtained in English politics, through the too great predominance of representative government, whereby the country sustains a loss of continuity and stability of legislation, and is tossed continually from conservatism to radicalism.

There are two Jacobite organizations in London, and although the revival of the movement in England only dates back a few years, its progress has been remarkable. One society is the Order of the White Rose, and the other is the Legitimist Jacobite League, of which the Marquis de Ruvigny is the President. The Marquis was in Boston a year or two ago, and it was largely due to his enthusiasm for the old cause that the Jacobite League was organized in America. My friend the laird of Highdudgeon is the head and front of the League in Boston.

The English Jacobite societies include members of some of the most aristocratic families in the kingdom. As might be expected, Scotch and Irish names predominate. The movement has also attracted many men of distinction in all the learned professions, who are naturally quick to perceive the charms of fantasy, since they thrive upon other people's illusions. There are thousands of men in all walks of life in the membership of these two societies, and they are both in communication with the head of the House of Stuart, which is at present represented in the person of Maria Theresa Henrietta of Bavaria, whose son Robert will, upon the death of his brother, the mad king of Bavaria, become King of Bavaria and informally King Robert the First of England, Ireland and Normandy.

It is whispered among Jacobites in Boston, and I repeat the rumor, because we owe so many of our agreeable delusions to Dame Rumor, the dear, wicked old woman, that the Jacobite movement has already attracted attention in the British House of Commons.

The Jacobites in America have no political aspirations. They are content to be a social rather than a political body, for this insures a continuance of both gravity and fantasy. Of course, they have their ideas

about the political machinery of our time;
but though their political ideas are revolutionary and reactionary, no good democrat
need lie awake fearing to be murdered in
his bed on account of them. It is unnecessary to state that whatever perturbations
the shadow of Jacobitism may have caused
at Westminster, the Jacobite representa-
tion in Congress is not causing the political factions in Washington much anxiety
at present.

It is believed among the English radi-
cals that the House of Lords is a hotbed
of Jacobitism. But in Great Britain,
especially among the more fiery-blooded
Irish, who from time immemorial have
fought for, and believed in, every impossible cause, there is perhaps more faith in
political miracles than there is among the
Jacobites we know. These ardent spirits,
who are the least tempered by philosophical Jacobinism, and are spoiling for a
cracking of crowns, are comforted with the
belief that the present deplorable state of
affairs in England, a wicked dominant
Parliament and a subservient Crown, will
find its logical conclusion in anarchy,
chaos and old night. And then — Prince

Robert of Bavaria will be haled from his obscurity!

But in general the Jacobites hug themselves in a martyrdom, which has the great recommendation of exciting curiosity and providing material for good, witty dinner-table talk, without any possible horrible exigency of a Bill being passed to sweep away their occupation by enacting the reform for which they are willing to perish,— but which they never want to live to see perish.

There are very few martyrs of public opinion who can ever hope to be asked out to dine at great houses. The Jacobins never have such good fortune, — at least not those who confine their Jacobinism to the unprofitable, although delightful, advocacy of the Devil in literature. Did any cabinet minister or government ever yet think it worth while to offer a philosophical Jacobin, with an eye on both sides of every question, a good fat magistracy? That is the ruin of many poor devils whose wits seduce them into Jacobinism; they are too philosophical to be in any wise formidable—except to their own party. They are too sincere to amuse the public, and too logical-minded to embarrass the workers in iniquity.

As the Jacobite movement exists today, it is the expression of the sympathy of the dilettante element in society, with certain aspects of the large general social movement away from the creeds and vicious materialism and commercialism of our modern civilization. There is little hope of any restoration to the throne of the Legitimate house in England, and a measure of doubt exists in the minds of some people as to the long-continued occupancy of the House of Brunswick. And so the Jacobite movement on both sides of the Atlantic really stands more for the restoration of some high ideals, and beauty, in art and life, than for anything else.

The Jacobites are, to some extent, Epicureans in philosophy. They are the cynics of idealism, and so, though in advance of the thought of most of their contemporaries in art matters, in America at least, they are only on the threshold of beauty, which is in the inner sanctuary of truth. Their idealism would utterly collapse if the prop of a comfortable and substantial surplus, for the luxuries of rare

prints and first editions and wines with a
genuine bouquet, were removed. Among
them are a few, a very few, choice spirits, who actually stint their stomachs to
indulge their passion for the beautiful.
But these are mostly the Jacobins, whose
Jacobitism is far more dubious than their
talents; men who are admitted to Jacobite
circles only on that shameful sufferance,
which wit and genius, outside the covers
of a book, in the poor, vulgar envelope of
God, obtain everywhere among the comfortable ones who inherit the earth.

But the Jacobites are certainly unique
among the Philistines of our comfortable
classes. Outside of the picturesque bac-
chanals in honor of the House of Stuart,
they cling to the pleasures of the mind,
and recognize that they are the highest
pleasures. No; that is wrong. They
recognize these as *their* highest pleasures.
We know that they are only allied to the
higher pleasures. They realize that such
pleasures must necessarily appeal to the
few; but they have become bitten with
some of the doctrines of the perverse fol-
lowers of Epicurus, and do not comprehend the futility and triviality of the pleas-

ures of the mind when wholly unimbued with morality.

The Jacobites have many things in common with the Philistines. They are dreadfully like them in one respect. Although they revolt from the established slavery of opinion, their patronage is dangerous to the arts. In making a fine art of fine folly they come perilously near making a folly of the arts, especially of literature. They, as well as the Philistines, come to love an army of good words, but care not greatly for real thought. I do not sympathize with making thought the sport of the few. It is as fatal to write to please a specific minority as to cozen the masses. The courtier who knows his King and Cardinal becomes their shadows and echoes if he remains a good courtier, but he is afraid to think aloud. It is as evil to think the thoughts, and to echo the prejudices of a class, as it is to try to sink to the intellectual level of the lowest prisoners of circumstance. There is, of course, more catholicity of opinion in highly-cultured minorities, because, cloyed with sweets, they often think more of the manner in which a thought is put than of the thought itself, and the daily game of critical battledore has taught them to regard ideas more as playthings than as realities. They are therefore but amused with heresies that horrify the bourgeoisie.

But nevertheless it is an evil state to play the mere revolutionary for mere revolutionaries. It is only when a haphazard shell from the workshop of some rough, passionate thinker comes hurtling into their midst from out of the noisy turmoil of the outer darkness that the æsthetically minded comfortables learn to perceive the difference between the thought of a man who has all the Epicureans and Euphuists at his fingers' ends and can play the acquiescent, amusing cynic to perfection, and the thought of a man to whom the sanctity of his thought is dearer than liberty or life.

To understand the true nature of thought, and the holy passion in which it is born, it would be well for Jacobites, and others, to turn to the divine fury of Milton's "Areopagitica." The philosophy of the Jacobites, in spite of its fantastic exaggerations and Epicurean complexion, is much more like that of the smug Philistines, whom they despise, than they suspect. Their favorite doctrine of *laissez faire* is one of the most cherished doctrines of smugocracy. The main difference is that the Jacobite version of the gospel is disseminated in delightfully epigrammatic prose, in beautiful, tantalizing limited editions, printed on stout buckram, with rubricated initials, wide margins and uncut edges; and the other is scattered broadcast in Blue-books, newspapers, and in the choice repositories of family literature.

There is, however, a palpable difference in the intellectual emotions excited by these two literatures; and, in the choice of two immorals, we naturally choose the most curious and amusing. It is this fact which attracts many men to the ranks of Jacobitism, whose occupation does not permit that audacity of opinion, which is born of indifference and a fat exchequer. As a delightful Jacobite said to me one day while we were on a debauch among the thousands and thousands of dusty thoughts in the crypt of the Old South Church, "I dare to say anything audacious and unpalatable, because I always say it so genially, and because I myself so seldom believe in the things I preach."

The Jacobite creed is, to put it briefly, *Credo quia impossible est.* But the Jacobites most emphatically disbelieve in any Utopia for all God's poor players. That is an impossibility which has no glamour for the Jacobite imagination. On the contrary, they are apt to clothe blind Chance, the poor harlot of human vanity and greed, in all the high authority of the highest divinity; and they cling to the comfortable belief that injustice, misery, suffering and the ironies of accident, are all divinely appointed to maintain the picturesque, and to minister to the gratification of the elect through the force of contrast. They believe firmly in the elect; and if the play in the world does really mean anything, it seems to support the good old orthodox idea of predestination.

If moral worth consists, as some of the ancient philosophers asserted, in taking pleasure in the intrinsically beautiful, the Jacobites are certainly more moral than some of the moralists who condemn them, for they take pleasure in beauty alone. It is pertinent to inquire in passing, to what baleful star we must impute the fact that most moralists have a fatal trick of making morality hideous. The Jacobites follow the old Pythagoreans in the belief that wisdom is superior to virtue, because virtue is a poor sublunary thing, while wisdom touches that purer, higher, spiritual region, where reason is wrapt in divine intuitions. But then, unfortunately, the wisdom of the Jacobites is almost wholly comprised in that fatal trick of paradox. A man who has a ready mind and a gift of words, once an adept at paradox, gives you all his store of wisdom in a few paradoxes; and then his career of miracle-working begins, and, with admirable and baffling skill, he summons into existence the palpable shadow of nothing. That is his miracle! The virtue of the paradoxical writer is this: he cannot leave behind him a whole library of his own works; such writing necessarily compels infinite polishing and compression. The trouble with Epicurean idealism is that it too fatally suggests the commonplaces of the comfortable life — beefsteaks and beer! There are some facts of life whose too deliberate exclusion but emphasizes their existence. The moral dangers of Jacobitism are shown in that observation in the "Pilgrim's Scrip" — "Poetry, love

and such like, are the drugs earth has to
offer to high natures, as she offers low ones
debauchery." But we touch in this society
a fugacious toleration, or indifference, that,
at least, has a curious eye and ear for the
charmed lure of thought; and as Meredith
says in the same book, "Culture is half
way to Heaven !"

Thus, in spite of its high-colored political background, Jacobitism is mainly a
literary and artistic propaganda, but it is
in no sense a reversion to the literary mode
and spirit of the Restoration. The literature of Charles II.'s time was, as our picturesque Jacobite most picturesquely put
it, an exaggerated revulsion from Puritan
and prurient ideals. The literature of
Charles II.'s time shows those excesses
which always follow a period of unwise
rigidity. But it was a transition time
without ideals; and the Jacobite movement
in America is essentially a movement for
the restoration of ideals in art, and a
reversion in literary and artistic expression
toward older methods of thought, and that
old freedom of philosophical opinion, which
belonged to a much earlier day than
Jacobitism itself.

Jacobitism is closely in sympathy with the Catholic revival and the renaissance of idealistic painting and literature, which is quite opposed in spirit to the gross literature of the Restoration. All these things and Jacobitism are more or less bound up together in the aims of the new schools of poets, painters and essayists, which include the impressionists, the symbolists, the grotesques and the rest. They most of them find a refuge from the purely materialistic background of their idealism in an exaggerated Euphuism.

The Jacobites do not recognize any affinity in their aims and those of the Jacobin wretches; but the interest of the Jacobins in all this is, that it affords an engine to a body of opinion in favor of moral and intellectual freedom of thought. It is rank heresy, but a good deal of the reality in the Jacobite propaganda is Jacobinism of the modern, moderate, intellectual sort, that abhors the cant of violence very much more than the virtuous respectables, who, indeed, soberly regard the constabulary as the last word of civilization.

"Oh world diseased! Oh race empirical
Where fools are the fathers of every miracle."

In looking over this budget of heresies, I should quake in my shoes if I did not remember that, luckily, heresies nowadays are the shuttlecocks of five o'clock teas, and for most men such discussions belong wholly to the world of abstractions, and so may pass without comment or contradiction. Even the man who is most wedded to the established, who has found imperturbable consolation in the sage advice of Epictetus, "The best way to be happy in this world is to want everything to happen just as it does happen," greatly enjoys a revolution *on paper* every morning at breakfast. But, "in action" as the "Pilgrim's Scrip" has it, "Wisdom goes by majorities," and I so shroud my political and sociological opinions and speculations in mystery.

ABOUT CRITICS AND CRITICISM.

———

I.

A MAN with a talent for leisure — a
talent as rare as many others held in
greater esteem — cannot help thinking it
was good to live in the "good old days"
(putting them in the eighteenth century),
if one only chanced to have deserved so
well of Providence prenatally as to be
under no obligation to deserve anything of
anybody in this world. When one's circumstances entirely remove all necessity
of deserving well of one's fellows, one
exercises unconsciously a strong moral
influence, for they at once become extraor-
dinarily magnanimous, and credit one
with all the virtues in the decalogue, besides many others not mentioned therein.
And it is to be noted, too, that these latter
are the virtues upon which the world sets
the greatest store. The biographies of the

deserving do not make very cheerful reading for those whose ambition it is to
deserve; but they must afford great
amusement to the wily ones, who have
learned their lesson of indifference, and
leave deserving to dreamers and fools.
Certainly the lives of the deserving in the
"good old days" can seldom inspire envy
in the deserving of these days; but, all
things considered, it is not very probable
that the deserving of the eighteenth century, if they were to revisit the earth,
would find any remarkable improvement
in the condition of their mistaken brethren
of this end of the nineteenth century.

If a man is so destitute of resources
that he can only hope to get his bread by
deserving it, he merits hanging. A man
can only become honored in the community by being dishonest; for men love not
qualities, but the appurtenances of power.
If it is love one seeks, there is at least one
way to secure it —become a feeder of
swine. The Prodigal Son had just found
a sphere in which he could be *loved*, when
he became a prey to the common desire to
be *popular* — a totally different thing. It
is not at all remarkable, although few

people are conscious of the fact, but we never envy the deserving. We may under the stress of certain emotions admire them, but we envy only the undeserving. We seldom envy men's qualities, anyway, but simply their conditions.

But there was a certain excitement (at least it seems so to us looking back into history) about the profession of letters, as about the stage, when it was a disgraceful outlawry, which is lacking in these days when it is a respectable, but poor and contemptible trade. There is not much to be said on moral grounds for the old system of patronage in literature, but one should hesitate before condemning it altogether. The present system is theoretically better, but a thousand and one deteriorating influences in the machinery, with which thought has been clogged since the invention of printing, and the practical abandonment of real schools, cause one to almost doubt whether we have made any real progress. The steam press has multiplied all the books that are mere printed matter, and this is such a profitable business that publishers do not care to venture the cost of genuine thought; and so in a world full of books, literature goes a-begging in the market-place.

Thus it has come about, that the modern tendency (in England and America, at least) is to flatter and appeal to the tastes of the mob, which never encouraged any art. It is certainly better to flatter one discerning individual (it *is* a discerning person who pays for flattery) and retain one's intellectual freedom in all other particulars, than to dilute one's self to flatter a multitude of fools. —to sell one's very soul for popularity. As Emerson said : " Popularity is for dolls." The old system of patron and client, with all its hideous incongruities, fostered some of the world's greatest thinkers. The popularization of the types too often perverts them to base uses, and fosters more than anything else the two extremes of the pious platitudinarian and the hysterical "society" female in literature.

Every great work of literary art has been written to satisfy one critic —the author! If everything had been written to please the public we should have no literature at all. The public is the damnation of all serious endeavor in art and critical litera-

ture; and the high priests of Clotûre are
the conventional critics.

In the precarious calling of letters, the
critics and essayists occupy the least stable
position; and it is with the art of Mon-
taigne, Addison, Steele, Dean Swift, Dr.
Johnson and Goldsmith in mind, that I
allow my imagination to revert to the old
days —the days, when, if Steele had to
write an article in the tap-room of the
Devil's Tavern and wait for a printer's
"devil" to bring him money enough in
return to pay his reckoning, and if Dr.
Johnson and Goldsmith got only garret
room and scanty meals in the households
of Edward Cave and Ralph Griffith for
their labor, they at least were not compelled
to cater to the tastes of the mob. They
were robbed, of course; but they were
not obliged to think the thoughts of the
tinker and candlestick maker. The abo-
lition of thought is one of the effects of
the complete commercialization of literature in these days. This is the triumph
of contemporary periodical literature.
Imitation is only possible to poor plod-
ding mediocrity. Thus we have produced
the interesting spectacle of our contempo-

rary literary world. The publishers offer the public the crystals of sugar loaves, but they refuse to give currency to diamonds. All the periodicals have a peculiarly distinctive character, and a certain organization of literary sparrows is always to be found in them twittering a different strain in each. It is the perfection of literary mechanism; but genius is more one-idea'd, and it cannot surrender its individuality even in the interests of conventional morality. Men can make wax flowers, but only God can impart the perfume to the rose and the narcissus.

It is impossible to give any rules for the production of *literature* by the industrious indigent or the socially ambitious, but one can give a recipe by which any person with a certain facility for misusing the English language, can obtain success in literature nowadays. Get a dress suit, go into society and dine The Editor — using the term in its generic sense. A man cannot provide himself with brains, when the Almighty, for His own good reasons, has omitted to furnish him in this particular; but most men can procure a dress suit, and it is a substitute that more than meets the occasion.

There are at the present time many earnest and true thinkers in certain fields of thought a little removed in the popular mind from literature, but in literature proper the ease with which all degrees of fools and quacks with golden keys gain access, makes the lot of a reviewer indeed a pitiable one.

There is a large class of publishers which insists upon modelling the opinions of authors, to make them appeal to an imaginary audience, which is conjured up in back offices, and whose existence is honestly believed in. And there is a still larger class of publishers that, with equal fatuity, sincerely believes that the public is shocked at honest criticism, and of all critical condiments has only developed a taste for molasses. The public has indeed a good appetite for colorless common-place, but its instinct of curiosity is as strong as its literary taste is undecided. It is as much through condemnation as praise that great books obtain any vogue at all. But, on the other hand, general condemnation of balderdash only gives it a wider circulation. It is absurd for the publishers to be so desperately anxious to

pass all their authors through a moulding-
machine, that turns them out like children's popguns which will all make exactly
the same report upon discharge. Of
course, the effeminate, the undiscriminating do not weary of these small noises;
but once you give masculine, robust boys or
men the chance to handle genuine pistols
and artillery, popguns lose their hold
upon their imaginations. The popular
writers and the popular critics have always
prevented the popularization of the great
authors; for popguns lose their significance the moment great field pieces are
brought on the scene.

The publishers are too much afraid
of offending their constituencies. Their
little catechism for authors is ludicrously
unnecessary, when one reflects that the
public is only deeply concerned about one
thing — its belly; and will read good and
bad literature without discovering a pin's
point of difference between the two.
Perhaps, however, in this view, I am
thinking of a distinct class of readers —
the large genteel class, which buys books
as it buys silver spoons, in order to
possess every appurtenance of a well-

ordered household.   It is probably nearer
the truth to say that the great mass of
the public has acquired its letters without
learning to read—that is, to read in the
real sense.   It pores over that class of
periodicals and books which cannot be
regarded as literature at all; and therefore, in a consideration of literature (even
bad literature), is not to be taken into
account.

The fact is, the position of the publishers is an impertinence.   They should
rightly be middlemen, authors' agents,
who put forth and distribute literature
without any power of interference in its
character.   Only fools buy books for the
imprints of publishers.   Thinkers buy
books to add thinkers to their circles —
not publishers.   We buy books, and even
magazines, to learn the authors' opinions,
and to get their opinions expressed in
their own fashion.   It is very good of the
publishers, no doubt, to attempt to exclude
from circulation any opinions which, from
their point of view, we may not agree with.
But it is precisely the people we differ
from that we desire to meet.   We discover
our   own   opinions   in   learning   other

peoples'. But for publishers' opinions, with all deference to a worthy class of tradesmen, we really do not care a tinker's damn.

Here is an exactly analagous case. We patronize a certain restaurant because the chef tickles our appetites with the diversity of his bill of fare. He is an artist; he lives upon popular suffrage, and we appreciate his art. But we do not desire the company of the proprietor of the caravansary at the meal we have paid for, and we do not care a fig for his views upon the art we discuss. All we ask of the publishers is the bill of fare; nothing more. But, perhaps, we cannot get what we are willing to pay for until the machinery of production is more simplified than it is under the present competitive system. We must wait until publishers are authors' agents, on commission, as are dealers for other inventors, before we can hope to buy literature in the market-place, which exists primarily as literature.

But the critics will not consider works published by the author, and the public is popularly supposed to share their distaste, for all the channels of reaching it are closed to the ·author who manages his own business. This plan has, however, been worked by John Ruskin in our own time, and has been found practicable, I believe, by several great French authors. Nobody is ever amazed that a brilliant statesman, or lawyer, or a great general is able to manage his own affairs, and there is no reason whatever to assume that literary genius can only exist in men incapable of protecting their own interests in the ordinary business of life.

II.

IN the good old days of Addison and Steele, and afterwards of Dr. Johnson, Burke, Goldsmith, and Sir Joshua Reynolds, a new book, or a new play, or a new journal was the talk of the town; and the criticisms which were made at Button's Coffee-House and at the Mitre Tavern in Fleet Street were the deliberate opinions of men who had time not only for opinions, but for reading, and leisure not only to read, but to think. The best criticisms are often those which fly across the mahogany after a good dinner has been disposed of, and when those around it are

poets and wits and philosophers. There
is a reconciliation between body and mind,
in such a moment, that is sacred. The
criticisms which arise naturally out of the
conversation of thinkers, when a bottle or
two in the window-sill transforms the
world, make the stuff of some of our best
literature. Their spontaneous birth gives
them a subtle character that the deliber-
ateness of written literature denies. In
the alchemy of good talk men surprise
even themselves—the sparkles come and
go, and tantalizingly elude and tickle the
memory the next minute, when the glasses
are filled and new bubbles rise to the
surface. In this lies their greatest charm.
We speculate about these gatherings—
with, say, Dr. Johnson in the chair; and
in imagination summon the wits back to
their seats—only to find the substitution
of our wit for theirs makes them very commonplace shadows indeed. The fact that
these opinions and judgments often died
as soon as they were born adds consider-
ably to our curiosity about them. Old
port and Madeira often played the mid-
wife upon these occasions. A gathering
of wits can be as dull as a convention of

deacons without a bottle or two of wine on the table; for wit and wisdom, as well as headaches and heartaches, are born in very small wine-glasses — constantly re-filled! It is one of the strangest of anomalies that out of the same bottle of port will come imaginings too fantastic for telling, much less writing, with the sanest criticisms upon life, philosophy, and the actual creations of art. (I am now refer-ring, of course, to the first bottle of port and not to the third.)

The critic whose criticisms are of any value should read one book carefully, and then think about it for a week. There is nothing more common and nothing more useless than the continual devouring of books without thought. Elizabeth Barrett Browning compares this form of mental dissipation to whittling. The critic should read and think and dine, for opinions, if not thought, come nowhere so readily as at dinner. ,

The poor critics have usually belonged to what Nathaniel Hawthorne called "the aristocracy of wretchedness." In the pop-ular imagination they are the autocrats of literature, and it is amazing to what an extent this delusion is shared by authors, to whom there is no mystery about a printing-office. The critics are the serfs of literature. If the authors have done with Grub-street, the poor critics have not. It demands a much more varied equipment and talent to write opinions that shall possess interest and originality about contemporary literature (the bulk of which is not worth the effort of making up one's mind about at all), than to write an average popular novel. A vivacious chronicle of opinion requires a wide acquaintance with genuine literature, a judicial, logical mind, a faculty for epigram, a strong creative power (using the word "creative" in its proper sense) and a distinct charm of style. The average popular novel demands none of these things. In fact, it would not seem extravagant to say that the average popular novel becomes so through the complete absence of these qualities in the creator. The critic who signs his work has usually a better sense of proportion and a deeper insight into the responsibilities of literature than the popular novelist who reviles him. The critic, at least, contributes to the literature of knowledge; while the popular novelist, with his industrious multiplication of mysteries and insipid heroes and heroines, simply denies his readers an acquaintance with literature of any sort. Anonymous critics who abuse their office to ventilate personal dislikes, are as unworthy of notice as anonymous letter writers.

But to be quite candid, only those critics who have an established place in literature and have forced the proprietors of the journals to permit the printing of their signatures, dare express sincere, honest personal opinions. As a matter of fact, speaking generally, a much less interesting custom than Donnybrook criticism obtains in our current literature. "Bloody" Jeffrey, Croker, Gifford and their myrmidons have no successors. The "Bloody" sessions are closed; and they were so amusing in their ludicrous, earnest asininity, that one cannot but regret that a little of their barbarism has not survived in our day of vapid, sugary criticism. The philosophic mind is merely amused at adverse opinion, expressed with exaggerated violence and intolerance. The literary claquers of to-day, who always yell one way like a pack of hounds, cannot afford one the same innocent distraction from one's serious interests. Honest criticism is almost a lost art; and so is the dishonest criticism that amuses. I confess if I had an hour for relaxation I would rather spend it in seeing a man hanged in effigy than in listening to one of those eulogies that are like eating-house dishes — all alike except in name.

After all that can be said in disapprobation of them, the critics are more to be pitied as the martyrs of ignoble machinery, than execrated as bad amusers. Are they not asked and compelled to sacrifice their whole intellectual capital to the mechanical approval or disapproval of a multiplicity of dull authors, who could not write an interesting paper on their own stupidity if it were to save their necks from the halter? We ought to be thankful that a few critics are able to dispose of their ostensible subjects in a paragraph or two and give us essays on other matters very much more amusing. A really independent mind will not allow itself to be fettered and padlocked by titles, even of its own forging, when it can find sweeter, greener pasturage in a by-path.

A man who has a decided taste for literature is entirely unfitted for the career of a succesful practical critic nowadays, as it is far more important for a success in literature to be a woman, a beauty, a possessor of a wonderful wardrobe, and give costly dinners in "society," than to possess any literary qualifications whatever. This makes criticism an impertinence. A woman is allowed by all the rules of chivalry to be a fool without danger or reproach; but a discreet woman will not publish the fact broadcast. The worst of being a professional literary critic is that you are brought into collision with so many fools every week — in gilt edges, cloth and paper covers. A man had far better ruin his palate as a tea-taster than poison the sources of his imagination and inner life as a literary taster. The average critic who is compelled to earn his livelihood by his pen usually exists in an atmosphere of hopeless contemporaneity. His examinations and his judgments in their very positiveness must necessarily be of the most perfunctory character. He is, with very few exceptions, in the same pickle as the unfortunate society reporter, who is obliged by his necessities to squander his life in the vestibule of "society," and hails every vapid young woman, who makes her formal entrance into her gilded cage, as a paragon of beauty and an Admirable Crichton in petticoats. The counting-house controls the critic's judgments, and allows him no selection; and, indeed, when an author or publisher has a social lever, as well as the ordinary means of influencing the opinions of the poor critic, through his employer, there is very little moral hesitation in evidence: then the critic cuts capers which may well make him desirous of preserving his anonymity. It is hard to have to praise a lady's book because she is the wife of a millionnaire, and one's employer is invited to her table; and it adds a new poignancy to the situation when the lady's dinners and not the book must occupy the chief place in one's review.

A man without imagination cannot be a critic — neither a true nor a sham one. If he were only allowed to say what he thought, the critic's life would not be so miserable; but his opinions are furnished him by gentlemen whose ideas of literature

are picturesque, to put it mildly, and the
poor man has to father all sorts of crudi-
ties, or else resign in favor of someone to
whom intellectual prostitution is less
obnoxious. Books, which should be
among the real satisfactions of life, become
the bane of his existence. Even when he
reviews good books he is in no better
plight, for he must not let a careful review
of one good book crowd out a dozen puffs
of twelve bad ones: and so he has to put
the same smear of molasses over everything which is thrown upon his table. He
is only asked to read enough of the books
that are sent to him to give his public a
taste of their condimental character: but
he has to read so many every day that his
whole existence becomes one long
nightmare. He is the victim of the thousand and one semi-weekly, tri-weekly,
weekly, semi-monthly and monthly libraries of fiction, and having leisure only to
know the names of literature, he is haunted
with a million multi-colored, grotesque and
often suggestive covers of the popular
sensational and didactic novels. Some
writers flout the poor critic for his misfor-
tunes. This is mere wanton cruelty. I

have an immense pity for the critic serving his term of servitude — possibly because I have served a long term at the galleys myself.

The secret of one-half of the ridiculous puffery of the press is poverty. The critics are often brilliant men of strong literary tastes, but they do not belong to themselves; they belong to a counting-house. It is owing to this deplorable perversion of the critical office that good books are so often neglected and allowed to die in a week with the bad ones. The indiscriminate puffing has led the mass of readers to disregard all criticism, which, whatever certain novelists may say to the contrary, rightly and honestly practised, is a very useful and necessary office.

But it is painful to dwell long upon the condition of the unfortunates under the harrow. It is pleasanter to turn to a consideration of a more legitimate and less saddening phase of critical writing.

III.

GEORGE SAINTSBURY, recently published A Code for Critics, which, while containing some wholesome counsel, taken too much

to heart would hopelessly divorce criticism
and literature.   It is a code for commonplace reviewers — not   for   critics; for
reviewing and criticism are two distinct
vocations.   Mr.   Saintsbury's   rules   are:
"Never   to   like   anything   old   merely
because it is old, or anything new merely
because it is new" (which is sound common sense enough, but not startlingly
original); "never to judge anything in
literature or politics except from the historical and comparative standpoint" (which
in respect to art would often prove to. be
pinching); "and always to put the exposition of the subject before the display of
personal cleverness."
    The greatest creative artist goes to
nature as if no art existed before him.   The
painter learns to draw from the *plaster cast;*
he expresses himself from *nature*.   It is the
same in creative literature; and it is the true
function of criticism in a consideration of
art to refer to nature as the highest standard.
Such a code is too cast-iron for the critics
whose names belong to literature.   It is
eminently good advice for the cataloguers
of literature — for compilers of text books
for schools, who need modesty; but other-

wise it can only satisfy those poor folk
who think they can raise the east wind
with a pair of bellows.

The body of great critical literature contains a very considerable portion of the
world's best thought; but the makers of
this literature suffered no self-effacement;
and examining and illuminating the work
of other men, while doing their own thinking, it must ever be borne in mind, that
they were essentially creators, and not mere
commentators and cataloguers. Indeed,
many of the greatest creative minds have
found expression in writings distinctly imbued with the critical and inquiring spirit
— men whom we cannot put below the
salt — and it is obviously impertinent therefore to beg a second place in literature for
such thought — much less to divorce it
from literature altogether.

There is, as a matter of fact, nearly always
something that is suggestive and attractive
in the work of the critic who consciously
strives to force the conclusion that he is
wittier and deeper than the author he dis-
cusses; for he may not succeed in his
attempt, and thus afford one a source of
innocent merriment; or he may succeed

(for there are instances of critics whose
light has dwarfed that of their authors
into feeble candle-light), and in succeed-
ing add to the sum of our pleasures by
merging criticism into authorship. Indeed,
there is very much to be said for digression
and discursiveness in criticism. To cite
but a few preëminent examples, men who
combined keen critical faculties with an
equally strong sense of personality, which
consciously or unconsciously permeated all
their essays, this ideal of personal subor-
dination was broken by Charles Lamb,
Thomas De Quincey, Heinrich Heine and
William Hazlitt—and who can doubt that
we should have lost the best element in
their essays if they had left themselves out
of them?

The only kind of criticism that is organic and inheres properly to creative literature, is constructive criticism; what I
may perhaps call inferential commentary—
the embodiment in a brief statement of
one's ultimate impressions, derived from a
chaotic mass of impressions received
during a careful and sympathetic reading
of an author. The antiquated fashion of
minute verbal criticism, while necessitating

great labor, is about as useful to us in our literary navigation as a chart of the waters of Mars would be to an Atlantic pilot. The best criticism is that which throws the man against the background of his time and its distinctive influences, and with as accurate measuring as possible, discovers his moral stature for that time, and other times. This consideration of an author rises to the dignity of literature itself. It is not the mere explanation of what is already clear, but is an illumination of some of the subtle processes which take place in one in reading, involving not only the intellect, but the conscience — a continuous operation of reconstruction — a perpetual reconciliation of antipathies, preconceived ideas and new sympathies and intuitions. This is a condition of individual development which, in certain highly sensitive and absorbent minds, often provokes the production of thought as distinct and quickening as the thought that quickened it.

IV.

THE æsthetic instinct in the race, in its crude form of love of color, fine feathers and beads, is next only in potentiality for good or ill to those other crude and vulgar instincts, which insure the continuance of the race and keep the world from tumbling into chaos — if we accept Schopenhauer's formula that "the world is simply the perception of a perceiver — in a word, idea." Herbert Spencer emphasizes the fact of the innate love of fine feathers as conferring distinction upon the wearer, and pushes the analogy into a consideration of the prevailing ideas and practice in regard to modern education.

There can be no doubt but that this desire of attaining distinction, is the impelling force in the production of that considerable portion of our literature, which, for convenience, we designate as *belles-lettres*. Its claims are not those of mere utility, but it is certainly not devoid of real use, for it develops certain faculties in us that are apt to get rusty from want of employment. It is a platitude that Vanity is the lever that has moved the world. It is a far greater force than hunger. While hunger is rifling bakers' shops, Vanity is making seers and heroes. Life without cocks' feathers is not living. Cynics, optimists, pessimists, fatalists — we all wear cocks' feathers in our hats and seek mirrors in the eyes of our circle. We pay very dearly for the wonder of our fellows.

But to return to our painted savages, and the humble beginnings of æsthetics. Herbert Spencer points out that decoration precedes dress; and cooking precedes civilization. "The facts of aboriginal life seem to indicate that dress is developed out of decorations." Thus, it is evident that the love of æsthetics, in some form or other, is one of the strongest factors in the social life of the most primitive states of society. The whole complicated web of our arts is held by a thread to the aboriginal love of color. And it is worthy of note, in passing, that, speaking generally of the mass, it is only in this crude form that the innate love of æsthetics exercises any appreciable influence in our modern civilization. But the taste exists, and has its root in instinct. It is not an altogether arbitrary matter of will, an ingraftment upon the simplicity of nature, but the development of a common and natural appetite. It is an appetite that finds only a strange and violent expression among the masses of people, mainly because, under the competitive system, they are entirely absorbed in the struggle for mere bread, and their consequent condition of mental and physical squalor affords no opportunity or desire for cultivation. Among the women it still finds sporadic expression in a barbaric love of color in their dress; but the generality of the men usually look at the world through the bottom of a quart pot. They are as reconciled to the sombre in their surroundings as undertakers' mutes are to funerals. This utter content with the ugly is, no doubt, necessary for the supporting of existence under such conditions, but it is one of the most dreadful things about the life of the slums to those who come in out of the sunlight. It certainly shocks the fragile daughters of the well-to-do who occasionally peep with pretty horror into these rookeries — of which their benevolent fathers are frequently the owners. But the savages of the slums often do not wash and have no money for paint, and so, having traced the analogy between the inhabitants of the wilds of Central Africa and those of the wilds of the Bowery, we will proceed with our argument.

The germ of æsthetics is in the crudest and most superstitious form of religion : all poetry begins in religion. The imagination is aroused and receives impressions long before the observation is sufficiently trained and enforced by a catalogue of comparisons to refer such impressions to Nature. A considerable gap in intellectual development separates the activity of observation and the activity of reflection upon observation — except the crudest and most perfunctory kind. In the natural order of things, poetry, in some form or other, precedes philosophy. Poetry is the firebrand plucked from the early camp-fire of barbarism to lighten the darkness of superstition. Its advent is the twilight of the world; and although the shadows it casts are often too grotesque to afford a clue to the times, with it begins history, and out of it finally comes philosophy. Poetry and philosophy should never be put asunder, for they are as akin as light and heat. Appreciation of poetry always antedates a knowledge of the nature and elements of poetry, just as men learn to use their voices in singing long before they are conversant with the systematized

laws of music. The introduction of measure into poetry and music, adds to their
beauty, and is as necessary as order is in
life; but in the application of these principles we must not forget that in their
essence they are arbitrary, and we must
not confuse mere conformity with excel-
lence. The subtle spell of poetry and
music cannot be analyzed; it escapes and
rises above all laws, which are but the
lathes and chisels of art. The tools are,
of course, necessary, but the perfected
work is the product of more than the will
and the tools; and the overplus cannot
possibly be defined, even by the artist, in
any less elastic term than inspiration.
We can tell how many miles an hour the
wind is blowing, but we cannot analyze the
weird color sounds of the music it makes
in the telegraph wires over our heads.
The beauty of the poem or the piece of
music is a fact to those whose minds are
caught in its gossamer toils; the analysis
of the charm may be dull or interesting, but it necessarily consists largely of
hypothesis. The secret of great art over-
lies the fulfillment of the laws of art. The
artist is bound to observe these laws, but

he is bound to do something more, or he fails of his purpose.

If this be granted, then it is clear that in the consideration of æsthetic art, the critics must not content themselves with an acquaintance with literature and the principles of art. And, on the other hand, they must be more than simply acquainted with the rude externals of life. The æsthetic instinct is like all others in one particular: it varies greatly in degree in individuals, and it is subject to the same laws of association, cultivation and neglect. In its highest development it reaches a plane, where, for all practical discussion, it loses all affinity with its origin. It becomes so infinitely refined and diversified, that what appeals merely to the elementary perceptions and passions, is crude, tedious and repulsive to the mind of the man, who has generations of refinement behind him, and whose æsthetic interests have traversed the line of mere instinct and taken on the complexion of psychological habitudes. At this stage of development, the mental and moral are inextricably commingled, and there is a large element of artificiality added; but henceforth the vision is colored by moral impressions and beauty loses its simplicity. A return to absolutely natural conditions and pure perceptions would, however, be much more unnatural and artificial. The crude instincts are greatly overweighted, but their dominance in the healthy, civilized man is intermittent, and they are seldom stronger than the imagination (which they so often seduce) when sustained by the ideas and habits of years.

It is therefore of the greatest importance that the arts should be practised to appeal to the highest natures and most cultivated intelligences, and never in such a way as to compromise with, or descend to, the intellectual level of those unspiritual or despiritualized elements in society, which constitute its principal ugliness. This, it seems to me, should be the basis upon which comparative criticism, in its application to the fine arts, should be exercised. The existence of the æsthetic sense or intuition, in a greater or less degree, in the mass, should make the critics unceasingly protest against its debasement by the panderers, who make their way into literature, as into everything

else. And by panderers, I do not mean
only those writers, who, according to orthodox notions, are supposed to cater to immoral curiosity, but the whole host of
popular triflers, who say: "The people
have only the heart to laugh and be
fools!"—and who are leagued together to
flatter and cater to the people, and keep
them fools. On the other hand, the existence of the æsthetic sense, even in a most
rudimentary form, in the mass, should
prevent the critics from rashly condemning
works of art by comparison with other
works of art, produced by men of oppo-
site temperament and under different
circumstances.

Every work of art, great or small, is a
problem in psychology. It touches certain chords of emotion and leaves others
untouched; and when a book does not
please us it is perhaps as often owing to
the absence of the proper sympathy in us,
as it is due to the lack of art in the book.
No matter how popular an author's works
may become, they cannot please every
mind, because, however excellent they
may be, they can only express relative
truth, and can only give us a glimpse of

beauty. Every man has a moral squint, more or less pronounced, and we all see beauty, as it were, in partial eclipse. The difference between genius and mediocrity often consists in the simple capacity of the former to trust to its own eyes, instead of looking at life through the thousands of other eyes that would perform the office. The greatest books do not always attract the greatest number of people, for they play upon certain chords that often do not exist, or are unresponsive from disuse, in the average man and woman. Then, too, however facile and pregnant may be an author's art of expression, it can never meet the demand made upon it by his feelings and imagination, so that for anything like an adequate interpretation of his meaning, his critics and readers must bring to his pages more than intelligence and knowledge of life and other books. They must bring the sympathy and the poetry that creates as well as understands. This is well exemplified in music, which is only a succession of noises to those who have no ear and imagination. A true book unconsciously selects its readers, as its author selects his friends and his studies.

Thus, it often happens that after a book has received almost unanimous rejection at the hands of the comparative critics, it gives pleasure and profit to thousands, who have escaped the blight of mere tradition, and have looked into their own hearts, and at life, for truth, and not for fashion. And if we accept the comparative method as our sole guide in a consideration of style, it is more unsatisfactory; for as there is nothing new under the sun, if a writer resembles another in his style of presentation, his works are without a reason for existence, and do not therefore call for any criticism at all. All men, being both isolated and dependent, capable only of limited sympathies, and incapable of more than the most partial self-knowledge, much less self-revelation, the mystery of life can never lose its hold upon thoughtful minds; and comparative criticism of the literature that must ever be the result, can at best only give us psychological hints of the impressions and conclusions of other minds. The value of comparative criticism lies in the broad generalizations it affords us, from an examination of the best minds on the most vital, if insoluble, questions.

V.

THERE is no ascertainable criterion of æsthetic art. All criticism is necessarily empirical. It is too often little more than an unfavorable opinion of Pegasus expressed by a man who is accustomed to riding only in an omnibus. A positive basis of criticism is impossible, but the comparative method of estimating imaginative literature, takes us farther away from a reasonable approximation, by comparing things utterly unlike, and rejecting those of most recent date for their dissimilarity. It rarely helps us to form any true and definite idea of the relative value of anything, for aside from conformity to the broad principles of art, there is frequently little community of purpose or method among the greatest artists. The tyranny of the literary conventions of the past has always been one of the strongest obstacles to progress in thought. On the other hand, to attempt to destroy the influence of the greatest thinkers of the past, simply because it is the influence of the past, is presumptuous and injurious; but when fresh examinations and the changes in political and social life bring about the

condemnation of old errors and prejudices, no matter how ancient and respectable, it is the lowest depth of mental ser-
vility to defer to the Tory spirit, that
always survives for a generation or two the
ideas which are effectually exploded by
the thinking men of the time.   But in throw-
ing away the conventions of other days
we are surely under no obligation to discard or depreciate the truth and beauty of
the art that grew up under their shadow.
We may disapprove of the whole spirit of
many books written in a different moral
atmosphere from ours, and yet experience
a keen delight in observing their beauties
of style and breadth of fantasy.

And we can be equally catholic in regard
to contemporary authors.   My friend, the
laird of Highdudgeon, is an ardent Mon-
archist, an aristocrat (and, it must also be
admitted, something of a snob), whose
ideas of sociology and political economy
are those of the fifteenth century; but he
has the gift of confidences, and his ego-
tistical confessions are absolutely fasci-
nating, while (and this is half the charm
of his matter) his command of beautiful
English is the envy of all his detractors,

among whom naturally he can number as many friends as enemies.   A fine old crusted Tory is very good company when one is desperately in need of relaxation, and does not wish to confess to a liking for clowning and ballet dancing, but he is a little too solemnly frivolous for one's serious moods.   Then there is Magnifico, whose ideas are all "advanced"—and borrowed; but whose heart is a mere organ. It would be wronging him to declare that he has no vanity.   He makes five thousand a year by frowning, and his judicial hesi- tation is so great, that his unexpressed dis- sents and endorsations have made him an honorary member of half the learned societies in both hemispheres.   His puck- ered lips carry more conviction than all the eloquence of his opponents.   He has a pro- digious conceit, but it is too silent to afford continual amusement.   He is so in love with platitude and is so decorous in his mental habits, that he will not even consent to be witty with other people's witticisms.   He always writes in a very restrained, judicial and correct fashion, but he is merely the proxy for his opinions and his gentility; and it would be to the decided improvement of his work, if he would only consent to err occasionally and express his own ideas. On second thoughts I perceive I am here guilty of a sad fallacy. I may affect a little contempt of Magnifico in his absence, but I am wofully conscious that in his living presence I cannot escape his ponderous condescension. He understands the value and impressiveness of dullness and a dignified demeanor in this world—but then he attaches a greater importance to its playthings than is possible for me. He casts a long shadow in the world, and is tickled—but then he never reflects upon the longer shadow of Death. There is nothing in the world really worth the effort of keeping up the farce of dignity. But Magnifico will probably never lose an iota of his dignity until he feels the cold creeping up his legs, and knows that he is in the presence of the arch joker, who rings down the farce a tragedy. But just think of the instruction in such a career, and the philosophic resignation one can derive from the contemplation of it.

Augustus William Schlegel defines the scope of comparative criticism as affording a clue to the conditions necessary to the creation of original works of art. He says:

"Everything must be traced up to the root of human nature; if it has sprung from thence, it has an undoubted worth of its own; but if, without possessing a living germ, it is merely externally attached thereto, it will never thrive nor acquire a proper growth."

This is the value of the best criticism. It compares the works of the greatest artists, not to discover conformity of opinion, or matter, or method, but merely to ascertain in a general way some guide to the highest expression of art. There will be almost as much correspondence in certain particulars as there is wide divergence in others, because, with all differences of temperament, and training, and experience, men of genius must deal largely with the same material, human life, and their reflections must often be of the same metal; but they are stamped with the superscription of their authors, and are as new as next year's apples will be. People do not discard a gold mine after the first few nuggets are discovered; and while life and death remain, literature can never become merely the echo of literature. In the examination of history, the sciences and philosophy, the strictly comparative method is indispensable to the reaching of any sound conclusions; although it is indubitable that, in the latter, essential truths have often been discovered in large and bold generalizations.

For the artist and the critic of æsthetics, however, the value of reference to existing works that have already met with acceptance, is simply that these productions have proved to contain elements capable of touching certain chords of emotion, and have therefore fulfilled the general laws of art, and are worthy of study as psychological hints. They are, to the artist, like Bædecker's guide books: they afford some indispensable information as to some things to be looked for, but they by no means exhaust the subject; and when the critics insist upon comparing all literature to literature, they are in reality finding fault with the Almighty for not moulding the mountains after the description of the guide books. They are comparing Vesuvius to the fusees that have been honored with its name; a glorious

sunset to the limelight at the theatre.   The
secret of great art cannot be weighed out
and sold in newspaper articles; but the
mystery of life is too deep for the plummets
of art, and so there can never come an end
to art — or not until the mystery is exploded.
The infallible standard is Nature, and
this forever eludes any systematization.
We do not go to an author to explain his
work, or to see if he conforms to another
man's ideas of art, but to gain something
from him which will clarify our own mental
atmosphere, and give an impulse to our
own thinking.

Other critics may differ from this — but
it is a fact that, whether we are wrong or
right, we remember writers through our
agreements   and   disagreements   with
their thought, and the final residuum of
gain of which we are conscious after the
effect of immediate impressions has lost its
original force.   We do not find the charm
of one writer to consist in imitation of or
resemblance to another.   We are, doubtless, oftenest attracted by our personal
agreements.   But our point of view changes
as we learn more from our reading, and as
our critical faculties are developed we

become at once more sensitive to impressions and less swayed by traditionary views and prejudices. It is the business of criticism to deal with ultimate impressions — masses, so to speak — and not with minor defects; and so, if an author offers nothing that is beautiful and quickening, it is not worth while to categorize his minor shortcomings.

VI.

THERE is small place in our study of literature proper for that kind of criticism which confines itself entirely to bald comparison, and alternates between the quotation of familiar passages, *en bloc*, and the perpetration of conventional labels. Of the latter, by the way, I have, safely locked up in a trunk in my garret, a large and varied assortment. It includes all the approved condescensions and humilities, and I am ready to sell it at a great sacrifice, or exchange it for one good book — even if it be but a book of proverbial philosophy, whose lessons consist largely in inciting one to the verification of its exceptions. The completeness and authenticity of the collection cannot be doubted, when I state that it was left to me by a great-uncle of mine, who, for many years, earned a precarious livelihood as a literary taster for the London Saturday Review. My great uncle was perhaps the glummest humorist of the whole gang of glum villains who wrote and write for the Saturday. He died scowling.

Candidly, I regard as the best critical writing that which is either avowedly or surreptitiously self-expression on parallel and on dependent themes, if such lead to clarity and definiteness. A self-obliterated critic is, to my thinking (it should be remembered that I am referring to literature in its narrower sense, and am not including history, philosophy, and the literature of physics), as satisfactory as a stale Stilton cheese, so economically hollowed out that only the rind remains standing. It possesses neither the interest of a ruin nor of a scaffolding. It merely arouses animosity for exciting an appetite without gratifying it. It is a poor empty cheat; it has even ceased to have a distinctive odor, but takes that of the viands nearest to it. You may pour rich, generous wine continually into its belly, and its poor spare ribs may retain some of it, but there is no substance to absorb it, there is nothing to ferment and ripen, and the wine, without changing its character, is obviously not improved in such a vessel. A good ripe blue Stilton, quickened with the best liquor, needs no apology for its presence on the table. And it needs no demonstration to prove that it is preferable to get wine from the wood than to drink it out of a stale cheese rind.

Certainly the time spent in reading scraps of an author, woven into a crazy patchwork, in which the critic's part is merely a thread of conventional opinion (of the impersonal, offensively-inoffensive, demure, and altogether damnable sort), might assuredly be more advantageously employed in studying originals. The critic who merely spreads his innocuous platitude and imbecility over the original soil, is not a quickening agency, but an altogether abominable nuisance. Only when a critic is himself original — a writer not merely of labels and echoes, but of views; a man, who, in his interpretation of others' philosophy, illustrates his subject with an experience of life at first hand — only the man whose thought is thus quickened by the thought of others, and who, in turn, quickens our thought, can be of any service to us.

When, in a consideration of creative art, the comparison is to Nature, we get the comparative criticism from which, in our own individual comparisons, we may learn something.

There are some preternaturally dull bigwigs, of very high standing in the literary world, who write as if they were muffled up in the shrouds of dead authors. They are ashamed of nature, and are as dependent upon precedent as police magistrates. They dare not look up and see God's sun shining in the heavens, unless some illustrious predecessor in their libraries made note of the phenomenon. They are afraid to compromise the dignity of the fancy figures they conjure up in their minds, of themselves, for the delectation of posterity. This is the only matter in which such men betray the smallest possession of imagination: they can see nothing worthy or beautiful in their own generation, but they are greatly concerned to impress a proper sense of their personal dignity and talents upon the hopeful children of their worthless contemporaries — if not upon those lost souls themselves. They despise their contemporaries so much, because, while looking back, they also look forward, and fancy they belong to no generation but to posterity. The dullest of judicial folk, perched upon the peak of bald precision, is secretly the thrall of a most grotesque imagination. "Folly is set in great dignity."

The man of great capacities and noble qualities can alone afford to unbend in general society. He is secure in the consciousness of his genuine purpose, and has his quip and joke regardless of immediate impressions. Dignity is more often than anything else a confession of weakness. Transparent, empty men assume it, on the principle that architects put stained glass windows in hallways that look out upon bricks, mortar and nothing, to give an appearance of depth and color. Where there is depth and flowers and color we do not need stained glass. Most men dare not be natural, for they would be discovered. Wise men sometimes assume dignity, because their experience teaches them that it is a needful weapon to keep fools at

an undisturbing distance.   A wit in a company of fools, is unanimously voted the
fool of the occasion.   A seer who unbends
to a fool for five minutes, is despised in
his neighborhood forever.

To-morrow is the Court of Reversion.
If posterity would only print all its por-
traits from men's own negatives, our literary galleries would be sadly monotonous.
But posterity will do no such thing!   It is
possible to cheat one's own generation,
but not all generations to come.   We have
much to be thankful for, when we reflect
that so many portentous negatives, handed
down to posterity, are ignominiously broken into fragments, or so reduced and
reconstructed, and printed in such colors,
as to give a delightful half pathetic, half
ludicrous interest to literary and historical
portraiture.   Dullness so often counterfeits
seriousness, and plays Pontifex, that it is
very gratifying to know that posterity
sometimes avenges its poor misguided
forefathers, knocks Gravity's black cap
ingloriously over its eyes, and banishes the
judges to limbo.

After all, it must always be remembered,
a critic is only a human being.   And who

is at once wise enough and foolish enough
to surrender his judgment and personality
completely, even in the presence of the
sages, whom he can summon at will in the
library? It is no more presumptuous or
unforgivable to hold up one's head in the
strong daylight of great men, than in the
fitful, ephemeral matchlight of one's
vague, or uncomfortably crowding and
omnipresent hobgoblin contemporaries.
It is healthful to be honest occasionally.
There is more to be said for the retention
of instinct than habit; and modesty is
usually merely a convention — a disguise.
Let us throw a little of our false modesty
to the winds (we do not want to wear masks
so long that we forget our own complexion), and get all there is to be got out of
the natural satisfaction of our sane appetites; among which, rightly understood, is
egoism.

SOME MASKS AND FACES.

I.

I AM the poor rebellious pawn of my
stomach. I am a buccaneer. But I think
I may say with modesty and justice, that I
only contrive to support the character at
such great violence to my whole intellectual and moral temper, aims, and inclinations, that I am sufficiently punished by
my own dismal exploits. A few of my
associates in the office of *The Sentinel* have
more .predilection for buccaneering, and
actually derive some ghoulish satisfaction
from their work—a horrible fact, which
puts all my philosophy and algebraical calculations for potential moral and spiritual
remainders completely at fault.

In the early days of my acquaintance
with journalism, after the first great moral
catastrophe of my awakening to the real
world about me, I tried to solve this delicate question of ethical remainders by the

rough, unphilosophic method of common subtraction: for I did not then fully realize that the agreeable custom of hypothecating one's moral nature for so many dollars a week, finally reduces one's moral nature, when one seeks to extricate it, or its fragments, in such an inquiry as this, to almost a hypothetical quantity. But with increased and painfully acquired knowledge of this ghastly trade of buccaneering, I found myself compelled to invoke the aid of the higher mathematics, or surrender myself to the blackest sort of pessimism. Of course my choice was the higher mathematics.

One cannot weigh off moral and spiritual consolations against intellectual disaster in a sentence or a paragraph, and so I will not open an inquiry into the measure of comfort I have obtained from my mathematical calculations. But, if on this complicated moral question I do not know whether desperation or compensation tips the beam, I am quite certain that I have no stomach for this farcical life of a bravo in the dark alley-ways of publicity, and "'tis my poverty, and not my will, consents" to any participation in this tragic masking. It is entirely due to the mishap of my having been born into this century, which has criminally perverted the printing press, instead of into either the seventeenth or eighteenth, that I have ever held the remotest relation to this miserable business of buccaneering. I have no natural affinity with cut-throats and Paul Prys, detectives and confidence men; indeed, I had much rather be a good honest Billingsgate fish-woman. I thank Heaven, I have too much robust egotism to take any extravagant delight in playing Tartuffe for the glorification of the freedom of the press. Indeed, I think it is high time in America for a John Milton to arise who shall write a companion to " Areopagitica," on "The Necessity of a Censorship of the Press; to curtail its unseemly License to a rational exercise of Liberty."

For harboring such seditious sentiments I am sometimes regarded with grave suspicion in the high and ludicrously solemn councils of this nightmare world; and I confess I take but an indifferent interest in its trivial and contemptible doings — except, that when I allow my mind to dwell upon them, even momentarily, my bile is so disturbed I am threatened with hypochondria.

I hope I may not be misunderstood in the following statement, for I intend to keep strictly within the bounds of ortho- doxy: but upon a certain point, about which my faith used to waver wofully, I am now, after many years spent in the brigandage of journalism, firmly estab- lished. I have not arrived at my conclusion through any of those seemingly irrational processes of conversion familiar at revi- val meetings; but by inexorable logic.

The newspapers and their peculiar intel- lectual and moral methods and influences are indisputable facts; and the immense prosperity of the newspapers, at the cost of the dwarfed mental and moral percep- tions of the masses, is perhaps the most portentous fact of this century; and there- fore the doctrine of total depravity is removed from the perplexed region of the- ology and is proved beyond all question.

But my associates on the staff of the *Sentinel,* and in the small noisy world of which it forms a part, with but few excep- tions, are absolutely without any real knowledge of me. They are only acquainted with the facts of my grosser and more apparent necessities, and my more or less perfunctory discharge of certain duties for the procuring of some of the necessaries of civilized life.

In this shadow-world, in which all play a part, and in which, by the way, the most grotesque intellectual pigmies cast quite portentous shapes upon the screen of the passing hour, we do not get any nearer intimacy than do men in the ugly collisions of intoxication. The shadows we throw sometimes exaggerate, though more often diminish, us; but they always distort us. At any rate this life, although it consumes my days, is not *my* life. These ugly necessities and these unspeakably distressing duties are not *ME*. I only begin to draw the breath of real life as the sun sinks out of our horizon to rise in another.

I am a distorted shadow, a poor disturbed ghost, all day long, and let the sun shine as it will, it cannot make a healthy, moral, human being of me during the hours from nine in the morning until six o'clock at night. Unlike the flowers, my heart only uncloses and pours forth its true human fragrance with the moonrise.

I take on a human semblance at the
supper table, at which we mix up good,
honest jests, with no wicked mendacious
sting in them, and poetry and philosophy;
and after a pipe and a book for an hour or
two, or perhaps a walk to the seashore, or
down the shadowy turnpike, which con-
nects my sundown suburb and the hideous
noonday town, I begin to be conscious of
human ideas and impulses struggling into
life within me.   And at last when the
workaday world and its claims seem to
have faded out of my memory, I enter into
that mystic world, whose mockeries I know,
but love to court.   I climb up to my eyrie
garret study, from whose diamond-paned
window I can catch a glimpse of a patch of
silver sea; and then — ah, if print could but
whisper it only in sympathetic ears, instead
of blabbing it to all the scornful Pharisees
of the literary world!— and then in spirit I
am a poet.

II.

I HAVE only thus hinted at my dual life,
because it is typical of so many lives in
this time and country, which are sacrificed

to the devil, in order that some tattered remnant may be devoted to the high and noble service of literature.

In touching upon my own experiences, I can write without any exaggeration of the poignant bitterness of the nightly and early twilight endeavors to balance accounts between the Mr. Hyde and the Dr. Jekyll of the forced partnership, which is the secret woe of perhaps a good half of the men whose names are more or less current in contemporary literature. And this is the reason for this hint of the secrets of my own midnight confessional. These horrors underlying our comfortable good-natured amusing literature, out of which all the coarse scum of the alley-ways are expelled, unless they consent to come a-masking *à la mode*, are usually hidden out of sight. But it is only to the honor of all who strive to make honest literature in these days of literary mumming that some facts should be known.

It is too bad to have to admit a worser man to all our most sacred counsels, and it is deplorable when we have to pamper this rascal with the sacrifice of one noble and worthy interest after another, because we

cannot deny that it is he and his miserable, heart-breaking charlatanry which
keep us in bed and board. And then,
too, what humiliation there is in the
thought that this villain, who degrades
us and makes our highest ideals and God-
given thoughts but a penance, is, after all,
not an utter alien in our brain, but sprang
up there native and lusty with the threat
of starvation. Of how many of our literary men is it true that the capacity and the
spirit was there, for better things, for real
work — but the cupboard was empty—*is*
empty!

It is unfortunate that for the most part
our *wants* crowd our *needs* out of our lives.
It is a condition well put in Ecclesiastes:
"Wisdom is good together with an inheritance, *and profitable unto them that see the
Sun.*" Unto them that see the Sun!—ah,
but what a mockery it is to be conscious
of that great inheritance of human pity
and love and tenderness, that poetry which
sets the soul free, and then to lose every·
thing in the horrible hazard of earning a
little bread and meat and shelter. Well
indeed may the poet in his despairing
moments sometimes envy the ignorance,

and even the besottedness, of the poor desperate outcasts of our civilization. Their
ignorance is their bane, but it is also their
protection from greater tragedies. For
these the world is beautiful in vain; and
this is Nature's partial compensation for
the havoc human nature makes. It is better
for such offenders that they hear no music in
the rustling of the trees, see no visions in
the clouds, catch no divine messages in the
break of the sea, find no peace or promise
in the sun-kissed, wind-kissed ripples and
eddies of the river — only see in the latter,
indeed, a last refuge from their kind. It
is better for such that, in the stifling and
perversion of the mind, those divinely torturing intuitions, which are insured to
some by the accident of birth, quickly perish, and forever, as far as this world is
concerned.

If a man's poverty is increased with a
faculty of spiritual vision that unfits him
for contentment and ignoble patience with
the moral decrepitude of the long servitude
of utility, in which he shares the portion of
the beast, he is indeed in a pitiable strait.
The world has no ears for poets and
prophets who come not arrayed in purple

and fine linen, secure in their contempt
of the world. Our stomachs may sometimes be consolers, but they rob the majority of us of all that we prize in life, of all
that gives beauty and sanctity to our lives,
of their very spiritual marrow. They
debar us from our inheritance ; we sell our
birthright for a mess of pottage almost
every day. But while the pangs of hunger,
and their anticipation, not only terrorize us,
but fret away something of the purpose of
the few whom God has made irreclaima-
bly poets at birth, it must be confessed
that they do also occasionally prove a
wholesome and necessary counterblast to
indolence, and compel the greatest to share
something of their incalculable fortune
with their fellows, in order to procure the
wherewithal to satisfy them. Still they
more often drag a genius from his pinna-
cle, and make a pot-boy of the poet.

"The mass of men," wrote Thoreau,
"lead lives of quiet desperation. What is
called resignation is confirmed desperation." I confess I see nothing in the facts
and conditions of our modern civilization
to induce any contradictory optimism that
would not be merely an emphasis of some

pervasive dogma of a very respectable and very dubious character; but putting the question of the masses aside (since certitude is impossible, and there is a pitch-and-toss chance of consolation for those who are shut up in sensation, which is denied to those who live in the spirit), it is quite certain th.t the man, who, from his youth upward, by temperament and instinct, has lived the inner life of the poet, is only reconciled to a lower plane of thought and life when he has lost all interest in what once made the world and men sacred and beautiful to him.

III.

It is a most lamentable thing that, in spite of all the literary activity and the intellectual restlessness of our time, there are not probably more than half a dozen writers in the United States who follow literature, pure and simple, as a profession; and it is noteworthy that among these there are neither poets nor essayists — the backbone of belles-lettres.

The men of letters of the old type who were concerned with more momentous

questions than Sandy and Arabella's love
affairs are apparently either extinct in this
country, or banished. Emerson, Thoreau,
Lowell, Whitman   and   Dr.   Holmes,
were   the   last   representatives   of   this
sort here.   Since their day we have had a
plague of literary little ones, who never tire
of telling us how well-behaved Sandy and
Arabella are in their love-making.   For
that good, lusty, robust wit we find in the
old English writers we seek everywhere in
vain.   It is severely disapproved of by our
Lilliputian literary dictators, who would fain
persuade us that purring is the thing.   But
oh, how some of us, in the crush of life,
long for that laugh and roar of the old
giants.   It is not that I have any quarrel
with the serene and gentle spirits, for these
never lacked convictions and vigor.   It is
only the hypocrisy of good temper that keeps
terms with trivialities of all kinds and laughs
with superior scorn at the great and tragic
and sober fantastic facts of life, and declares
they exist no longer, that makes me
regret I cannot command all the catgut I
could put to a good use in a merry hanging
Monday.
    I can only recall the names of a few

novelists, who, without fortune, solely dependent upon their own efforts, are able to devote themselves to the life of letters; and among these, I regret to say, the most prosperous, the men whose undivided devotion to their calling is the least doubtful, are gentry (and we must make the term generic to include the ladies,) whose productions are unmentionable and unreadable, through their crude lubricity, and who bring literature itself into bad odor among the ignorantly moral. Within recent years there has been a very marked increase in the publication of this sort of vile pandering, and it has brought into suspicion a certain necessary measure of freedom in art, which could only be a helpful influence in the direction of moral sanity and both Christian and sweet Pagan love and sympathy.

This new audacity of those on the fringe of literature is, in its way, a sort of protest against the indifference of the better classes, or, at least, the people who have the means and leisure to broaden their horizon, which has forced nearly all the literary impulse of late years in this country into alien and subterranean passages.

The higher types of men, however, bow to the inevitable, and since they cannot follow the native bent of their minds without incurring the perpetual temptation of so befouling their intellectual and moral integrity, they go into one of the professions, or some commercial pursuit, and make literature their recreation — their hobby-horse.

If they are wise they will not be deluded into imagining they can find a compromise in journalism. Indeed, I believe that a man, if he is not utterly lacking in the temperamental qualifications and habits of mind necessary for executive work, will not only find the daily round of duties in some commercial occupation, more dignified, less irksome, and less exhausting, but in every way more interesting and pleasant than any of the menial offices of any of the lower forms of literary employment can possibly be. Under such conditions Charles Lamb produced all his best work; and, from what scanty experience I have had in a dreary life of literary brigandage, I can well believe that men of some serenity of temper can find a distinct relief in the multiplicity of business details, and,

too, in some sort, a fillip, through the force
of contrast, for the less arbitrary interests
of their leisure.

At any rate, the literature thus spontane-
ously produced, out of the overflowing
heart and mind without regard to popular
demands, editorial whimsies, ephemeral
excitements, and the strain for novelty in a
crowded market, is more apt to be unvexed
art than that of the poor devil whose pen
is forever in the ink-pot, and who is in
more danger of immediate and material
ruin from his possible excellencies than
from his most determinate and palpable
deficiencies. A man can indulge every
whim that makes good literature, when he
does not have to ride his hobby-horse to
catch "editions" and early mail trains, and
perform feats over "scare headlines"; and if
he never does get into print at all, he, at
least, has had all the riding.

But the poor journeyman is under a constant strain to put away all those elements
of culture, mental integrity, natural feeling, logical faculty, and imagination, which
combined make style and literature; and
he reluctantly subdues all his real interests
in a continual effort to echo the echoes

that chase each other through the vapor-
ous minds of those "all sorts and conditions of men," for whose high pleasure it is
continually alleged the abominations of the
half-hourly newspaper press are committed.

The man of affairs is seldom so busy,
unless he is greatly bitten with the social
mania, but that he has his *heures perdues;*
but the man who innocently goes into journalism under the hallucination that it has
some sort of intermittent relation to literature, sells his soul to the Devil; and, to
make matters worse, with so little pru-
dence, that after a precarious life in a brigandage, which does not even procure a
share of the spoil, he ends his days in the
gutter. At forty years of age he is an old
man, and there is a superstition in the world
of journalism that only beardless boys make
good brigands and cut-throats. At any rate,
one never sees a reporter who has definitely
emerged from the thirties, and there are
no fortunes made in this cut-throat business,
except by the highly respectable owners of
the bravoes.

Unfortunately, however, the majority of
men of literary instincts and temperament,
are entirely without any executive or busi-

ness capacity. I do not think shrewdness and common-sense incompatible with the possession of genius; and there are examples in the range of literary and artistic biography which prove that genius can be allied to all the most admirable qualities of Scotch and Yankee thrift; and these even practised, for self-preservation, until they touch the point of niggardliness. Turner, for instance, in his latter years became almost miserly. Carlyle had the sturdy Scotch peasant's genius for the thrift that keeps mind and soul secure and independent. It is by no means the least of the virtues. It is often the only power that can save a man from the long servitude of expediency and mental and moral dishonesty. But nevertheless, it is perhaps more often the case that, in the exact ratio of their imaginative and creative endowment, poets and thinkers and artists are lacking in all those qualities which are essential to securing success or even a livelihood in the practice of law, medicine, teaching, preaching, broking, political prophecy, or tipstaffing.

In the intense competition of modern life an indifferent teacher or lawyer or clerk soon goes to the wall. Many of the

most fit are crushed out at forty, for in
these days, we have got into the habit of
regarding forty as dotage.   Therefore those
miserables with only one talent, when they
are possessed of any decided moral sense
and proper pride and independence of
character, which forbid them sinking into
a complacent career of more or less suc-
cessful literary mendicancy and adventur-
ing, are compelled to sacrifice their hopes,
talents, ambitions, high sense of honor and
justice, happiness and comfort, to seek a
hazardous independence in journalism.

In these days, when almost every avenue
of literature is blocked up by men who
are merely literary manufacturers, with a
most plaguey passion of industry, there is
always great peril to the writer, whose literary aims are purer and higher than perhaps either his capacity or his conscience
would seem to warrant, in the alternative
that may present itself to him at a certain
crisis in his career.   He can either con-
tinue a hopeless struggle in poverty against
the tide of popular demands and the
forces leagued and mortgaged to popular
opinion; or he can risk the hazard of end-
ing poverty in a jovial confession of pov-

erty, and, turning his back upon the prizes
and discipline of poverty, adopt the large
elastic beliefs of a literary Franciscan, and
become a genial pilgrim among the well-
to-do and comfortable classes. Then,
making a jest of all such crude moral
obligations as can be cribbed in common
arithmetic and usurers' purgatories, he
can play the philosophic clown for those
cliques, which affect singularity, and have
so much discrimination as to pay more for
the court of such an amusing cynic than
for the flatteries of good honest tradesfolk.
These circles are perhaps as yet too small
in this country for the proper encouragement of all those writers who have a more
decided faculty for the production of beautiful and fantastic literature — mere literature — than for the practice of that formal
morality which is enforced, with many
pains and penalties, upon mortals of less
extraordinary endowment; but there are
signs of a continual social expansion.

If this sort of philosophic clowning (putting morality and that bigoted sense of self-
respect for one moment aside — and I
protest I have not lost sight of them, but I
must for one brief moment be catholic!)

was good enough for Shakespeare's fools,
it is possibly not such disastrous and un-
blushing wisdom in our modern poets.   At
any rate, almost every literary man has
some good politic friend in his acquaintance, some worldly sage who understands
the strange whimsies of the world of busy
men, one who always sells fresh fish in
Lent, and is ever ready with the well-meant
advice : " *Go, mountebank their loves.*"
And to be really charitable, if Nature has
included in our parts any blessed and comfortable strain of sophistry, we must not
be chary of exercising it.

IV.

IT is not every man of letters who possesses either the scholastic acquirements
or the temperament necessary to fit him for
the duties of a professor of literature in a
university, even if there were chairs enough
to go round ; and not all professors of literature, perhaps very few, can find in their
intimate chronological acquaintance with
literature just that overmastering urge to
self-expression and creation which, deep
down beyond all the plummets of compar-

ative criticism and culture, is the metaphysical basis of all literature.

Athough some very eminent men in the
long roll-call of fame have occupied profes-
sorial chairs — from Erasmus to James Rus-
sell Lowell, it is the exception for writers to
combine in anything like equal degree the
critical and creative faculties, and so by far
the greater number of those who contribute
to what we call the belles-lettres are wholly
absorbed in their one great passion.   If that
fails them, they have but the one resource of
perverting their gifts to the base uses of
literary brigandage.

In America it is true that the colleges
and the churches have afforded employment that was not wholly mentally and
morally dissipating and disastrous to some
of the most eminent poets and thinkers,
whose genius has redeemed the civilization
of this country from the charge of mere
industrial barbarism; and we may thank
Heaven that these havens from the plague
of popular interests have existed, or more
men of genius would have been broken on
the wheel than there have been.

The biographical dictionary of American
authors, with a few conspicuous excep-

tions, is more than anything else a record of poor devils whose talents were wholly perverted, and whose lives were wrecked, by the accident of having been born into the wrong hemisphere.

Every man who is truly called to litera-ture is not as surely called to learning, and usually has an instinctive abhorrence of theology, and as for the law, the average poet and imaginative thinker is apt to regard it as the sum of all villainies. In passing, let me say, however, that such an opinion is generally caught at a tangent from a more or less perfunctory contem-plation of the lawyers. There are fasci-nations for the speculative mind in the philosophy of law. And therefore, if a writer is not one of the favored of the gods, who cultivate literature upon a patrimony, he is thrown upon the mercy of the vary-ing tastes of the public, and that in a purely commercial community means infi-nite woe and degradation. And then, too, not every man, even when he has enough versatility of talent to accept the situation and live two lives, is content to appear before his fellows in a mask. His large overbrimming personality may be opposed to his more dubious talents, which, indeed, if too much indulged, would certainly imperil those very qualities and capacities which he made such sacrifices to save from overwhelming destruction.

The majority of writers, however, have little choice in this matter, as they are incapable of dividing their attention between literature (or, when they get wrecked, its immoral counterfeits and distortions) and any other pursuit. There are metaphysical hindrances which, after all, are as valid as mental or physical ones; and though the relation of literature and life must ever be intimate and unescapable, the poets and thinkers, irresistibly elected, will always constitute a Brahminical element in society. Even in our modern democracy there are more or less vague indications in some quarters of a revulsion toward that healthy government by minorities without which, in all intellectual and moral matters, every nation is in danger of stamping itself in history — imbecile.

In the beginning of this reversion from the poor clipt literature of the market-place and the brutalizing domination of vile and illiterate newsmongering, there will natu-

rally be more or less intemperance and
over-emphasis, some misleading revival of
finnicking art, some mediocre mediævalism,
and perhaps a flourishing bedevilment of
Euphuism; but these will only be temporary phases; and, though in the nature of
masks, since they do, at any rate, encour-
age independence of opinion and a diversity of observation and influence, they lead
us circuitously to sanity and freedom and
dignity in literature.

We are perhaps already upon the threshold of this new era — in the shadow of
the Euphuistic revulsion from more deliberate and unforgivable platitude. Its most
ludicrous manifestation is the invasion of
literature by those merely fashionable wit-
lings of both sexes, who, in the economy of
nature, should be content to circulate their
second-hand witticisms and observations in
ordinary social intercourse, and not go
outside their proper province, which should
be that of consumers and not producers.

If this craze of authorship among the
comfortable classes is, however, a sign that
our "high" society is not really all stomach,
but is actually beginning to grow a head,
we will suffer the infliction with becoming

patience.   But we pray that the wrath of
God may not be upon us forever.

V.

IT is exceedingly difficult for even the
most versatile of men to belong to two
radically different worlds, antagonistic in
fact, and keep his identity separate and
distinct in each, particularly when to
remain in one at all he must completely
forfeit, or, at least, put aside, his mental
and moral integrity.   Yet this is precisely
the miracle that thousands who are compelled to find a meagre support in journalism endeavor to accomplish.   They try to
combine the character of the mountebank
with that of the poet and thinker and
teacher.

The most tragical circumstance about
the horrible business of newsmongering, as
we see it in this country, in its most
degraded and most impudent form, is not
so much that it panders to the lowest elements of society, but that its huge vortex
swallows up and debases and strangles so
many fine, generous, noble natures, who
might perhaps have made the world better

for their having been in it.   And the newspaper makes of them what — what, in the
name of God?—poo*, self-disgusted intellectual bawds, tragical students of the
tastes of thieves' kitchens and dens of
infamy.

In case some amiable and virtuous knave
in the great world of journalism, who
finds the society of thieves' kitchens quite
congenial, should imagine that I am not
qualified to write upon this matter, I may
say I have spent almost my whole life in
newspaper offices, and have served in the
ranks in every capacity, and I write out of
the bitterness of a full knowledge.

We ought to make shrouds out of these
sad and dreary sensational newspapers!

These are some of the masks of literature, and none can tell what tragedies are
hidden behind them.   The true, honest
faces we seldom see; they are mostly banished to the very purlieus of literature.
The American man of letters is an imp of
letters after dark.   When he is the bond
slave and bravo of a newspaper he has not
only the difficulty of having perpetually to
try and forget the one world when in the
other, of re-creating the essential atmos-

phere in each, but he has to fight against nature if he would ever accomplish anything worth doing. I have known hundreds of good, gentle, noble men who were bravos from high noon until two or three o'clock in the morning, who, upon coffee or quinine, to keep nature from utter insubordination, were poets, priests, and philosophers from two until six.

But every book written under such circumstances costs *a life*. And then, no matter how fine was a man's equipment for his work originally, if he would belong to himself he must not belong more than half the time to the Devil. The ogre of the newspaper office is behind his chair, nay, in his ink pot, all the time. He tries to banish the noonday criminal in vain. After a few years in the masked service of journalism, even the most robust talent is crippled and deformed; and for men who are lacking in vanity, doggedness of character and the most intense concentration and tenacity of purpose, a year or two as a journalistic cut-throat is enough to wholly corrupt and falsify their talent forever. "The dyer's hand is subdued to what it works in."

There was a time when journalism was
in some sort an apprenticeship to the
higher forms of literature, teaching several
important lessons. But within a quarter
of a century the whole character of journalism in this country has changed. Even
the ideals and standards of Mr. Jefferson
Brick have been ruthlessly destroyed. Jefferson Brick at least had an ambition to
teach an effete and corrupt civilization
something of the glory of this land of political freedom. He a little over-estimated
Jefferson Brick, that was all. But our contemporary journalism does not belong simply to the pot-house, it is of and for the
bawdy house. In no country in the world
has the divorce between journalism and literature been so complete as it has been
for some years past in America. The
amusingly Jovian dignity of the old journalism proper is a thing of the past; but it
is supplanted by newsmongering of the vil-
est sort. Thirty years ago some of the
best and greatest names in American litera-
ature were associated with the journals of
the time, and some of the highest American literature was first published in the literary departments of the journals, It

was Horace Greeley who encouraged Thoreau in the *Tribune*, and Thoreau was no sensation-monger. All this is now over. Instead of 'literature in the so-called literary supplements and Sunday newspapers, we have snippets of news and vulgar trivial gossip about the domestic life of the personalities of the prize ring, the stage and politics. And we must not forget that literary abortion — the omnipotent American "funny man," who, in its ghastly antics, is more tedious than " Punch " itself.

All writing in a literary form which is impermanent by intention, is sheer perversity. What is impermanent in the arts should only be so from inherent weakness, and not intention. Every writer should write with all the fervor and labor necessary to insure permanence, whether he can indulge the hope and vanity of fame or not.

THE FASCINATION OF NEW BOOKS.

I.

THE fascination of old books has been celebrated by hundreds of pens. The names of Dibdin and Isaac Disraeli at once occur to one's mind as two of the most familiar and pre-eminent of orthodox bibliophiles, as one sweeps the department of letters in which this subject naturally arises. But almost every essayist in English literature has told us something about the resources and consolation afforded by a well-selected library of old books. Dr. Johnson, Burke, Goldsmith, DeQuincey, Hazlitt, and other writers innumerable, have paid their respects to the great dead, with whom they have held silent communion. One of Charles Lamb's most interesting essays treats of the delights snatched from old books at the booksellers' stands in the nooks and crannies of London,

between the old East India House and
Charing Cross.

But I do not recall any paper that
touches upon the charm of absolutely new
books. And yet almost every book lover,
who is genuinely a lover of literature, will
experience the constant fascination and
temptation of the potentiality of new books.
I have purposely implied a · distinction
between a lover of books and a lover of
literature. It is one of the strange quirks
of our imaginations, that we often come
under the influence of the appearances
of books, while we remain wholly impervious to the ideas they contain; as men
seek the society of the wise (when their
genius, if not their teaching, is recognized
in the circles of authority), and love to
boast, in other company, of their intimacy
with poets and philosophers, with whose
teaching their whole lives are at variance,
and at whose unpractical character they
often openly scoff. Thus there are thousands of good folk, whose social, political
and religious orthodoxy induces a corre-
sponding Toryism in taste, which never per-
mits them to feel curious about what is
growing on the other side of their tradition-

ary fences; but who, nevertheless, industriously amass great libraries (and often write about them, too), and invest all their follies with the dignity of high authority. But these are usually mere lovers of "editions" with no true reverence for books at all.

In spite of frequent disappointments, the real lover of literature is provoked into an uneasy curiosity, that feeds upon delay, by every thoughtful, suggestive title he sees in the book-shops, or in the book publishers' advertisements, and every new name which emerges from obscurity, with a rumor of the true associations about it, tempts him to extravagance, and ofttimes to very real sacrifice.

Every book buyer has solemnly vowed a thousand times to begin immediately to put into practice a much needed policy of retrenchment; but I never knew one, upon whom the habit of book-buying had well fastened, who ever succeeded in practising strict economy in this one particular. Lots of book buyers are parsimonious, and often miserly, in all other matters, but they will not quake even at the possibility of the Bankruptcy court, when they have set their hearts upon possessing a certain author.

We writers should thank heaven for the existence of such men — they are rarely writers themselves. But more authors read books than the tradition will allow; although perhaps it is more raiding than reading.

Indeed, I once knew a literary man with a love of books, who left his wife one morning to entertain a sheriff while he went out to try to collect some debts for some literary journeyman work done ages agone. God wrought a miracle in his behalf! He succeeded in finding a publisher tender-hearted enough to pay something on account for the work done. He started for home in triumph, — and returned laden with old and new editions, *penniless.* Even his poverty did not satisfy his curiosity about his contemporaries; and poverty is apt to make us discuss our contemporaries a good deal and read them very little. He had been inveigled into an auction room, and the sheriff, his tearful partner and her admonitions, all had vanished completely out of his horizon.

We are always on the alert for the new prophet; but our insight is less than our curiosity, and we have usually a poor discernment of prophecy. On the other hand, we do not always keep our heads when we read those works which come with the stamp of authority, and so we often allow solemn dullness to impose upon our native judgment.

It is a common mistake of a certain class of critics and writers upon literature to assume that only the frivolous minded are subject to this curiosity about works just fresh from the press. The envy of the learned serves them in just as good stead as the curiosity of the vulgar. The masses have been shut out for generations from all awakening influences. They are but now getting together some rudimentary mental furniture to aid them in groping for their souls, and it is true that they fall, and very naturally, an easy prey to certain forms of literature, which are but forms and no more. The masses are not anxious about thought just molten into type; they have at present ears for words only. But let us try feeding them on ideas for half a century before we despair and become wholly reconciled to the vulgar diablerie of the newspapers.

Those who comprehend the thought of yesterday will be but too anxious to discover prophets in their own day. The denial of this by certain critics, who cling to the skirts of literary orthodoxy, because they are naked, is without significance to any one who has a real passion for literature. The diffusion of this vulgar error by these persons is due to the fact that their acquaintance with books has landed them in that apathy and indifference usual with the custodians of libraries and clerks in book-shops, who merely know the names of books. A new volume of Herbert Spencer is just as intrinsically important and valuable as would be the discovery of an unexpected manuscript of Aristotle. It is, in my view, quite as important that Herbert Spencer should live to complete the series of works which is to embody the thought of his lifetime, as that some archæologist should live to dig up an iron chest filled with old Greek tragedies, long supposed to have gone to limbo. If the *find* was a bundle of comedies we might hesitate, for there is much good philosophy in good comedy.

Those who are vitally touched and awakened in their contact with the great minds of all ages are conscious of the arbi-

trariness with which God orders their
thoughts, altogether independently of
worldly circumstances or happenings,
and so they do not despair of to-day. I
suppose even the most despondent of
contemptuous Tories does not care to
prophesy what the Almighty will do for
to-morrow. For my part, I do not believe
the world has at any time been empty of
great souls and great poets; and so I open
the most inauspicious looking volume with
respect. It is, at any rate, possibly the
best expression of a man, his highest ideas
written in his most divine moments.

But I do think the world has often
belabored its poets into silence. We are
all so in love with our ogre of "circumstances" and the tributes we pay to it,
that we have no sympathy for those, who,
having no stomach for such vulgar self-
diminution, die in the gutter silently contemptuous of our pot-bellied god. Perhaps
some very great poets, finding the world
so topsy-turvy, have not thought it worth
while to reveal themselves to the maskers
around them. It is scarcely a hopeful task
to preach truth in a world whose symbol of
government and society is the indifferent,

stony-hearted sphinx. We are the play-things of a false Fate, and the deluded never forgive those who dare to declare the farcical nature of the delusion.

An appreciation and comprehension of the beautiful and profound in literature, as in life and nature, inevitably forces us to the conclusion that the clue to the mystery of life resides in something we have not, and can never hope to discover. Until the invisible mechanism of thought and love and passion and hope is revealed and explained by the physicists, every new philosophy and every new singer will influence our imaginations and fan the undying curiosity of the race. If the knowledge of our limitations forbids any prophecies, at least it increases rather than diminishes our passion for examination, and so the rumors that envelop every new · thinker at once provoke our curiosity, and compound for our previous disappoint-ments and loss of faith in our kind.

If we are ever disposed to fancy that we have the secret of God's universe under lock and key in our private libraries and national museums, we should get some intellectual barbarian to figuratively but forcibly maltreat us. This is a poor sort of vanity.

One of the prime uses of such a great, original nature as Walt Whitman — a *man* in a generation, for the most part, stifling in a clothes closet — is that he shakes us out of this small, arrogant humility to make way for dignity and truth. We should remember that in attributing omniscience to the old writers, we are merely seeking to assign an arbitrary limit to God's mysteries, so that we may, by rendering due homage to "The Golden Age" (the accredited and final manifestation of the divine intelligence stirring men's souls to poetry), awe our own generation into silence or cringing deprecation and humility, and so secure ourselves in the poor dignity of a barren honor in a barren day.

But the poet who, living outside the jurisdiction of literary legislation, and totally ignorant of its statutes and penal records, simply listens reverentially to the whisperings of God in the fields and in the market place, and afterward publishes an echo of what has thrilled his heart and soul, at once establishes the right of to-day to take its place among the infinitude of sunlit days. The new thought should have as proper a claim upon our respectful consideration, or at any rate upon our politeness, as would a stranger from another planet, who certainly might be expected to possess one or two secrets worth listening to. Every new poet is a pilgrim and an alien.

When one considers that vanity is the mother of blind Toryism (among other evils), one wonders a little at this denial of all grandeur in our own time. The old-fashioned Tory is a pessimist of the most pronounced and anarchistic type. He would destroy all the interests of his fellows because they have multiplied the interests of his forefathers. He wants to put us all into short frocks because Adam wore an apron of fig leaves. He deplores to-day because the hands of the clock have moved; but he forgets that the hands go round. He forgets that genealogy and its spirit is not the concern of poets. They have, of course, had forbears but fortunately hold these vague gentry of less account than themselves and their songs. It is poor human nature to take more interest in one's self than in one's literary godfathers. But the desperate Tory cares little for human nature, and he will have nothing to do with the new book because Jeffrey, or Gifford, or Lockhart did not review it.

In this matter most of us have outgrown our terror of jack o' lanterns somewhat, and we should have an immense deal of irreverent fun with the "Bloody Assizes" of literary criticism if it were held to-day. I, for one, would love to have a good tilt with Gifford or Croker, or any of the other solemn autocrats of respectable Tory dullness. I have egotism enough to think I should grow fat in laughing them into modesty — and I have never been able to get any flesh on my bones. But we only have our little revenges and vendettas in literature because they so often afford material for amusing " copy," and not because we are so entirely lacking in philosophy as to be unable to recognize their ludicrousness and futility. Heaven forbid we should take them seriously.

II.

THE habit of buying books, it must be suspicioned, has almost fallen into desuetude.

Indeed, in spite of the multiplication of public libraries, one might almost say that the reading of books is becoming a badge of eccentricity, and is regarded by the generality of men, who swallow the news and their meat and drink together, as a certain evidence of an unsound mind. We want our literature in small doses. For this reason, the craving for variety has made originality almost impossible.

There is perhaps more "study" and less reading of literature to-day than has ever been known since the invention of printing. The hourly issues of the newspapers have created a factitious appetite for mere words, which is a more effectual bar to all thought, education and appreciation of the true realities of life than mere illiteracy. As long as the newspaper takes the place of the book, the work of the schoolmaster and the minister of God is in vain. In the homes of the masses in the cities we too often look in vain for books; and the talk of our young men and women largely consists of the idlest repetition of catch words. In the country, where men live away from this intrusion of hourly "editions," if we do not find many books, and seldom many of the greatest and truest ones, at least we are often struck with the independent philosophical conclusions of these simple folk. Ideas are an excellent supplement to a library, large or small, and if they happen to be the genuine offspring of true instincts and intuitions, they will compensate for a very great deficiency both in the variety and the quality of the books one reads.

The most magnificent public library, with its infrequent and soothing snatches of human sounds, its book-lined, dimly lighted alcoves, inviting meditation, — although these possess a distinct charm, — cannot, in my opinion, rival in allurement the old-fashioned bookstore. The library in a way anticipates all your appetites at once, and so leaves you with a feeling of satiety and oppression before you have broken your fast. But the book shop has enough to tantalize you, though not enough to make you despair. It holds an incomparable delight, with its opening and closing doors; its buzz of conversation; its piles of new books, — their virgin souls pressed between covers of all imaginable shades of color (often alas! to remain unfondled and unthumbed, although pressed upon those who come without opinions); its narrow passageways between stacks of books; its dark recesses, lit with ghostly gas jets, and its characteristic groups of habitues. The customers of any other kind of store usually all seem to be very much alike; but in a bookstore, one sees at a glance, all seem to have and to wear naturally, without accentuation or apology, their well-marked peculiarities of pose and physiognomy. Faces, whose vacuity we do not notice in a butcher's, excite our curiosity and wonder in a bookstore.

But perhaps the best place to read a book — old or new — is in a bare garret, where there are no other books or pictures to distract one, and where three flights of stairs impose silence between one and the world as effectually as the path to a mountain top. I cannot understand how a man could be the custodian of a public library, or even the owner of one of those splendid private collections (whose main purpose seems to be to make the lips of penniless book-lovers water with anguish), and write or even desire to write. Such a multiplicity of authors and subjects indeed is very seldom conducive to helpful reading.

But still it is easy to be wise in such matters, when a great deal of the attraction of books, new and old, consists in one's inability to buy them. A great many book-lovers have read much through the lack of pence which prevented the purchase of all the books they wanted. Possession would have deferred their curiosity and so ruined them.

There is a good story told of a certain bibliomaniac who when he wanted to refer to a book in his immense library sent out and bought a new copy. He lost half the charm of book-buying for his books did not represent any sacrifice.

Occasionally a good deal of the fascination of a new book is that we may one day meet the author of it, and so come into vital touch with the complement of the work. But if we reap anything from the book, it is usually fortunate for us that we cannot meet the author. Of course, in reading the old authors, although they are new to us in turn, this danger is removed (at least in this world); and as we all love a spice of danger we regret the loss of this element of attraction. It is this craving for a glimpse of the individual behind the thought, that makes us all so love biography, and, even more, autobiography. I suffer agonies every time I see advertised a new volume of memoirs, the price of which is beyond my resources. There are moments when our heartstrings seem to be wound about our purses; but, be it remembered, hearts are only concerned with empty purses! It is so seldom one meets a Man in everyday life, that one thanks Heaven for the happy phenomenon, which makes most men tell something of the truth, when they strive to reduce falsehood to truth's complexion on paper. The truth gets into our inkstands as well as into our cups. It is because our daily journals are mostly written in lead pencil that the truth so seldom slips into them.

But I, for one, am so nearly a spendthrift in my intellectual hospitality, that if ever the newspapers take to filling their great sheets with thought (even if it is only witty, dainty sophistry), I will gladly give up some of my precious hours of recreation to the reading of what this very morning has to tell me of the wonders of the last twelve hours. It is not that our newspaper press is so utterly deficient in morality, that pains me, so much as the fact that, it is so variously dull, and so irremediably stupid and vulgar. This is largely to be attributed to the conspiracy of wickedness which robs all journalistic writers of their independence by forcing anonymity upon them.

I flatter myself I am one' of those who can receive a positive good, and not feel any necessity to diminish my benefits by comparing them to those I already possess. Therefore I give the same welcome to the new book which teaches me something or pleases me, that I accord to the old book which performs the same office. I confess that I do not care whether the printer's ink is wet or dry as long as the ideas are in it. To me all books are new, until I have got my heartstrings wound about them; and then every time I open them they evoke old memories and new thoughts, with every turning of the leaves. My reverential curiosity about every promising new book is perhaps apt to be more an arbitrary matter of a mood than it used to be years ago when it was a pure instinct; but still, how-

ever sporadic it may become, I am sure I
shall never entirely lose it. If ever I do,
it will not be that I am either wiser or
more discerning, but simply that, wearied
in my passion for truth, I have buoyed up
my self-esteem by a conservative exclu-
siveness. It is one of the worst evils of
old age that it is apt to account for all its
increasing mental and physical failings by
the rapid declension of the race morally
and intellectually. It puts all its faith
in old almanacs.   .

There is at least one author whose books
will always be sure of generous attention
at my hands, even if I live to become a
nonagenarian. That author is myself.
But there are other contemporary
authors, whose works, apart from this
peculiar circumstance, really have a
stronger hold upon my imagination. Of
course they cannot so closely touch my
sympathies.

I can discover an excellent reason, without
any difficulty, for a new volume of essays
by that delightful egoist, Robert Louis
Stevenson. Augustine Birrell and William
Ernest Henley, too, have each a charm-
ingly original style, — almost an anachron-

ism in these days of the triumph of the "article" mode of writing, and a fine old feeling, quite eighteenth century, for essay-writing. We want all their books upon our shelves. A new novel by George Meredith is an event in many lives. I am catholic enough in my literary tastes to enjoy the fine touches of Andrew Lang's delicate humor and bantering Toryism; although I confess I think a little more catholicity would be to the advantage of his literary morals. His style is the delightful quintessence of dilettanteism. But there is a sort of bantering more intolerant than Calvinism. I have dipped enough into Walter Pater, to know that he is preeminently a stylist, with a delightful indifference about what is going on in the world to-day. And what does it matter since to-day is only repeating unnumbered yesterdays? I cannot rest until I have, at least, had a glimpse of a new book by Oscar Wilde, for he has an exquisite gift of paradox, and paradox makes us all sit up. Besides paradox is the half of truth, and the one half is surely as good as the other. With one half the truth provided for us surely we can contribute the other half ourselves. It is a chance to test the truth within us.   I do not believe, anyhow, that one can have a genuine love of truth unless one is somewhat susceptible to the beauty of sophistry.   And then I must confess I read more for amusement than anything else.

As my taste in letters is essentially masculine I do not know much about the work of that sex which is, or should be, the poetry of life.

I am consumed with curiosity about every new work I see announced upon ethics, metaphysics, and philosophical socialism ; but I regret that my ethics are too ridiculously antiquated to enable me to obtain possession of my favorite books through any less uncertain and troublesome method than that of barter and borrowing ; and so my philosophical library is restricted to a few inherited volumes.   But I console myself with the reflection that much of the best philosophy is contained in the works of the poets, — and in our own hearts, if we keep them young and merry, and open to all God's creatures; among whom, in our Transcendental moods, we can sometimes include humanity, in large and sufficiently remote and vague masses.

But when one tries to recall a few of the

names even among one's contemporaries, the mention of which excite a pleasurable anticipation, they all slip out of one's memory. As Walter Bagehot says, "The fact of a book being a book goes immensely in its favor." I thank heaven that ignorance was not omitted from my patrimony, for as long as I live I am assured a vital and enduring interest in books. And some such interest as this gives us a perpetual consciousness of our higher selves, and so lends a dignity and purpose to lives poor and insignificant enough in performance.

The man with a hobby-horse seldom commits suicide. I have haunted the book-shops for years without a penny, and I shall never make away with myself, as long as the privilege of fingering the new books, and dipping into them, is accorded me upon the old conditions, viz.: that I purchase a copy of *The Literary Guillotine* every time my head is in the basket.

A RHAPSODY ON MUSIC.

THE maestro has bowed and glided noiselessly to the grand piano. The hum is broken with a momentary hush, then rises again with hurried force into a wave of commentary, until pierced with a tremulous note demanding silence.

A minor chord or two follows, floating like a benediction into the body of the great hall, misty in the struggle of the incandescent lights with the waning light of the afternoon. It is the right light for music: one does not want a glare to dream in. A hush falls immediately upon the audience. The expressions on the upturned faces change rapidly, as if an angel had swept through the room, and in his flight had stolen the masks with which these "civilized" barbarians conceal the human in them. Music alone can compel this complete revelation of the human — this rare lighting up of men's faces with divine wonderment; music

alone can create of a sudden this intense
isolation in the midst of a crowd, that per-
mits, and, indeed, enforces, this supreme
abandonment of the imagination, this lib-
eration of the poet imprisoned in every
man's heart — this incontinent retreat
into the riotous world of dreams. It is
indeed the maddest, divinest of arts;
none other can evoke this marvellous
transformation of hard, worldly, animal,
indifferent, selfish and careworn faces
into beautiful, human faces — the faces
we look for in the streets in vain, and
lovingly welcome in our day-dreams.

Sculpture, painting and literature
sometimes hold us in their thrall, and, indeed, the latter is often the record of the
sister arts; still, they cannot dominate our
every fibre as does music. There is no
draught which can intoxicate more
quickly than subtle harmonies. Music is
our sport, and we are its sport: listening,
we live all the lives we hoped to live in
our early dreaming; and then live again
the life we have lived — thus hovering
ever betwixt the heights and the abyss,
we taste the distillation of all joys and
fears and miseries, and finding a sweet-

bitterness in all, we are delighted to be the playthings of this false Fate. All realities become the unrealities they are; only the ideas laughed at in the noisy streets outside seem valuable, and these are at once a consolation and a torture. Music makes us forget all things; and it brings everything back to memory. ·It flatters and mocks us; it lifts us up among the gods; it thrills us with power; it loosens a chaos of song diviner than any sung by men; it whispers of easy accomplishment on the morrow; and then drags up those yesterdays we thought were forever buried and reminds us that there is no morrow. It is the echo of our own hopes; and we, poor, fond fools, willingly accept its voice as an external certificate of worth and capacity; and, dreaming of that morrow, we are happy. Ah well, it is good to be happy — and what else can make us so?

After life and sunshine, music is the divinest, sweetest gift of God, who, to the ear attuned, graciously vouchsafes innumerable harmonies, even in the rattle of machinery and in the roar of crowded streets. But, of course, there is music in the shock of men; for music is the universal consoler, and life is music. All Nature throbs with music. If it were not so, this would be a world of madmen; for every rustle of the wind in the trees, every wash of the breakers on the beach, every cry of the birds, every sound, would come like a blow, torturing all the senses at once.

Listening to the music of Mendelssohn, Beethoven, Chopin, Wagner, Schumann or Schubert, one enters a new world— a world entirely strange to most men; and yet no man, once across the threshold, ever feels unfamiliar in it. It is the world of dreams—the mystic closet of the mind that every man possesses, but of which so few keep the key. The poet, the philosopher and the painter escape their poverty in this world; and all have separate keys. But most men, in the absorption of prosperity, throw their keys away. They are the poorest of poor devils; for dreams alone are real. One dreams, loses, and gains all there is to be gained. The other grubs among the muck-heaps of the world and gains much, but loses the secret of happiness. The only almost universal key to the gate of dreams, so rarely

opened by the mass of men, is melody;
and so the poet and the trader occasionally pass into this magic realm together.
But the former would never credit the
latter with any familiarity with it; and
the latter could scarcely describe his
acquaintance there. It is only by intuition that those to whom this is the real
world of their lives can discover their
fellowship in this workaday world: for
the world of dreams is a world of intense
isolation; and in this outer world the
dreamers may be *dreamers* to each other,
but they cannot possibly be dreams; and
the only satisfactory companions of a
dreamer are those of his dreams. Therefore the spirit world of music is like the
great silence of death; it has a thousand
entrances, unseen, stumbled upon only in
the dark—and every man must enter
alone.

Music is the confessional-box of the
whole world. If one has a dormant conscience one fears to awaken, one should
never go to a grand recital, for one is
caught in the toils of sound, and stripped
to one's self before one is aware of it.
True music—and I allude to that kind

only — is the arraigner of all cruelty, greed, pettiness, all misliving. It is the very poetry of passion; but it preaches a morality as rigid as the Decalogue's. All the grosser elements of a man are subdued, indeed, quite forgotten, under its spell. The man who would become the prey of his baser passions immediately after listening to a Beethoven sonata or a Mendelssohn march could (to use a paradox) never have had the patience to listen to such music at all. In the exaltation born of music one drifts naturally into introspective and heroic moods, and one is shocked to recognize one's littlenesses and meannesses in sudden hushes, or borne upon a wave of sound that sets all one's nerves thrilling with noble impulses while one is wholly unconscious of any physical being. But although music is an accuser — a conscience, that will not be swept aside, while it is throbbing in the air — it is also a great inspirer, a wellspring of worthy and human promptings.

Music is not only the world's conscience; it is the world's comfort. One can find all one's moods, one's hopes, and one's failings and fears in its great heart, but one can find forgiveness also. It is the mother of great resolves and good resolutions, innumerable: and perhaps, if in our workaday world we lived to a continual accompaniment of sweet and bitter harmonies, men and women would be less indifferent, less selfish and less cruel; in a word, not only human, but humane. The fundamental problem of life which confronts all reformers of existing abuses — the insoluble question: how to reform human nature — might then be disposed of. But, I fear me, if there were any intermissions, the looting, the chicanery and the brutality would break out with renewed violence; and so my panacea for the pimply body politic is no more practical than those of the *Sans-culotte* political economists. Of course, in the woods, among the hedgerows, and along the seashore, the air is filled with God's music, and one can draw up a sane philosophy of life with it ringing in one's ears; but in the cities where a clatter of men's wheels and engines has been substituted for God's eternal music, such a philosophy would seem quite insane. And yet, for the poet, there are doubtless eternal mean-

ings even in the recurrent, unceasing rum-
ble of a city's traffic and trades. The
music of the woods may be sweeter at
some seasons, but the music of the streets
is sadder, for it is the music of birth and
life, misery and wrong, short-lived gayety
and suffering and death; and still "the
loom of time" roars on, and each generation repeats the same old dirge — and
each thinks it is a new thing!

Every orthodox Christian dreams of a
heaven where symphonies and chorals
shall be unceasing; and perhaps this is a
vague recognition of the fact that music is
the most effective check upon the instinctive savagery of mankind. A heaven without music would be an immense anarchy.
It is certain in this world that hearts
which are quite indifferent to suffering,
misery, prayers and pleadings, and bitter
tears wrung from other human hearts, will
soften in a few moments, as Mendelssohn
whispers of a higher, diviner life. If men
had but usually ears to listen, the music of
the streets should have the same effect;
but, alas, it more often happens that the
roar of the great tide brushes any passing tenderness out of the heart, and the

noblest badge of the noblest manhood is condemned as unworthy *a man of the world*. What an ironical phrase that is!

The musician is less and more than a poet. He is less in retrospect; he is more as long as his art holds us in its sweet torment. He is the creator of a shadow world in which the poet may revel, but which no words can describe. Music is a universal language; it is foreign in every land, but it needs no interpreter. All Babel can listen and comprehend, but no tongue can translate; for music is idealized sound, and something more; it is the soul of all philosophies, all religions, all strife, all peace, misery and happiness. We have grand poems and sonorous prose in our literature, but music is the only art possessing pure harmony that is at once ideal and common. There is something lacking in the grandest poetry, something indefinable, that is in every snatch of true melody; it cannot be explained or accounted for by theories or laws, but poetry may make mere moralists or even better men; music makes demi-gods. To be able to pile sound upon sound until it reaches a grand culmination of triumphant or despairing music is to be able

to create, not only a few men and women —
the triumph of the novelist! — but a whole
world of marvellous peaks and seas and gods
and goddesses: it quite transcends the
delight of making beautiful English.

The world of the musician is entirely
different from this world of reality, but it
throws a startling, unescapable light upon
realities; it is the world of romance, but
it presents the realism of improbable
dreams — and what can be more realistic
than that? We delude ourselves with
"realities." Thought is the only real thing
in the world, and though we can enter
through our hearing alone, music is essentially a world of thought. All other pos-
sessions and pleasures are mockeries.

The musician holds the keys to human
souls, long locked; and, though he cannot
look therein, he does more — he throws
them open to those who would fain shut
out their cries and memories. And he
gives all who care to listen the freedom of
that ancient Eastern city of dreams, which
exists in the mind of almost every man,
and far transcends in mystery and splendor
the Orient men go out in ships to see.
Looking into the stolid face of your neigh-

bor you can scarcely think it conceivable
that he is floating in a garlanded barge,
lying on a bed of roses, with his head in
the lap of Venus, stricken with the languor
of love, drunk with the singing of the Bac-
chantes dancing at the prow, a King of
love and life—floating idly beneath an
amethyst sky, on a gently rocking purple
sea, broken into wreaths of pearls by
splashing nymphs.   But, good, respectable
citizen and lying butcher that he is, your
fat, red, smugfaced neighbor is actually in
the highest of bad company; and his stu-
pid-looking spouse, who, lacking an ear for
music, lacks all that excuses her existence,
does not know that her husband is a con-
queror in the Court of Love itself.   And
he, poor man, will awake, and go home
sad at heart—and perhaps grumble at his
own beefsteak!

Music is a great paradox: it gives and
denies; it consoles one for what is done
irremediably, and makes one yearn for that
which is unattainable; it laughs in one's
face at one's success, or ennobles one's
failure, and while comforting, dazzles one
with triumphs beyond one's reach;   or
else one is caught up in the grandeur of

the music, and wakes only to failure when the last note has died into silence, and the released hum of humanity — the disillusioning murmur of life, mocks one's new born hopes. Music makes life more real, and dreams more vivid than life. It is the gate of Paradise, and the cheat of all mankind; it brings supreme fulfilment, great desire, or great despair; it is everything to every mind; it is the echo of thought and the germ of reflection; it can be a queen or a common paramour. It is the one art practiced of men which completely transcends humanity, without being repellent to the lowest intellect.

Music is the sea on which all the argosies of our hopes go safely into port. It is paradise to the sensualist and the ascetic. All can find in it what they seek. The poet who sees visions and dreams, but has to write for his bread, and so cheats all the world, listening, sees his page crowded with great thoughts. The artist sees his canvas start into life. The merchant, forgetting his counting-house and ledgers, lives again in the wonderland of his boyhood, when he, too, dreamed of being a poet. All who are disappointed in life are crowned with success, or made content with the revelation of the cheat of success.

In the mad world of music old faces are seen, cold lips are warm and return one's kisses, old hopes are renewed, old loves prove true. Faces filled with joy are dashed through a rent in the sound, as the air is still quivering with the crash of a *fortissimo*, and then in the minor chords become contorted with pain and disappear. The audience and the hall are swallowed up in the vague shadows of this world of sound. Here are demons, nymphs, strange lights and stranger shadows — a medley of the most grotesque imaginings and human memories. The wildest imaginations of men find expression in music, as they never can in words or color, for music is both; and miracle of miracles! the men who cannot understand the mysteries of the world of books, set forth in plain types, are immediately in sympathy with this stranger world of music. It is a world of sorrows and joys, of laughter, joyous and terrifying, and tears of happiness and despair. It is the epitome of human endeavor; the mockery of human accomplishment. It is God speaking to men through his human agents.

If all this is madness, take a fool's advice: Go and be mad for one evening — and live!